Foreword

Some books add to our knowle⟨ ⟩ ply inside us, and this is one of them. ⟨ ⟩ ulties as much as facts, invites us to ⟨ ⟩ interplay of Self and World. Perhap⟨ ⟩ ancestors first signaled that encoun⟨ ⟩ back so far, takes pictorial consciou⟨ ⟩ ing to consider the conceptual thinking which defines our present ⟨ ⟩

CW01499348

The early Greek philosophers were still wrapped in myth. Contemplating cosmic origins, the fiery Heraclitus declared that 'thunderbolt steers all things." Others thought Water or Air more likely... each to their temperament. As for the author of this book, he lifts those elemental qualities into his discourse. Through his sprightly asides, anecdotes and skills in storytelling, he introduces us to a range of sages: the 'snub-nosed" Socrates posing questions in the streets of Athens; Plato (who had a nose for archetypes) admitting only geometers to his Academy – onwards to Augustine, Aquinas, Bacon, and beyond.

The writer's former law studies then prove useful in directing our attention to the essential gestures of their philosophies, while his interest in etymology gives glimpses of earlier forms of consciousness. If, for example, we translate the Greek 'a-lethia" with our blunt word 'truth" we miss both the reference to 'Lethe," river of forgetfulness, and the sense that we come to knowledge through 'un-forgetting." So, beware of assuming that our forebears experienced the act of thinking 'just like us." John Thomson's well-tempered thunderbolts will shake such lethargies from our heads.

Readers are sure to appreciate how this 'lover of wisdom" addresses them directly, sharing his doubts, his questions, and a lifelong search for meaning sparked by the writings of Martin Buber, which gave him 'a foundation in the essence of being human." Concepts of goodness, beauty, and truth that he once found lifeless became vital catalysts for creativity and free thinking in the classroom. Such was his dedication, teaching in Steiner schools for over twenty years and then, at Emerson College, training teachers in the art of education. 'Un-forgetting" was Plato's mode of learning. John Thomson's is more attuned to Aristotle's, 'moving towards future ends," ways of knowing to be realized through practice and in each moment. There is one thing that in recent years he has rediscovered – his love of painting and poetry.

Paul Matthews

Prologue

FOR ME THIS BOOK HAD its beginning a long time ago, in the years that followed World War II. In 1948 Ronald Gregor Smith, the translator of *I and Thou* by Martin Buber, gave a lecture on the book at the university where I was studying. After the lecture, I bought a copy of *I and Thou* and was immediately taken by its message which seemed clear at the time: a relationship with another was not just a question of psychology and chance. A few years later, I encountered Rudolf Steiner's *Philosophy of Freedom*, which raised for me the question of the nature of thinking. These two philosophers are prominent in shaping the contents of this book. I realized that the pursuit of philosophy is not like any other form of inquiry, whether scientific or psychological.

In 2006 I gave a series of talks tracing the development of philosophical thought from Plato to modern times. Some of the talks were given in the local pub. Audio recordings made at the time became the basis for the written version. It has required a thorough reworking of the original transcripts to make this book. I hope that the journey I have undertaken can stimulate in the reader a similarly rewarding voyage of discovery and reflection.

This book is not a history of philosophy from Plato to Buber. It is rather a personal journey and an attempt to show the different ways of thinking that philosophers have adopted in building their world-views. For some the starting place is in the mind with reasoning and introspection. For others, observations in the world of sense impressions provide the point of departure. Both activities are usually present but in different proportions.

The selections I have made and the comments I include belong to my journey. My purpose is to lay out a broad canvas of possible avenues of inquiry. On this canvas we find the earnest, diverse, rich and profound

The Experience of Thinking

Plato to Buber

Printed with the support of the Alkion Press Fund

ISBN: 978-1-7366829-0-6

First Edition

Printed in the USA

Published in 2022
by Alkion Press
14 Old Wagon Road, Ghent, NY 12075
alkion-press.com

Title: The Experience of Thinking
Author: John B Thomson

Cover photo by John B Thomson
Design and layout by Roman Kuznetsov

Illustrations by Megan Thomson Connor

The Experience of Thinking

Plato to Buber

John B Thomson

ALKION
PRESS

To my dear Marie-Claire

Contents

imaginings of thinkers intent on researching the meaning of the universe and what it is to be human.

In my study of the philosophies I have been guided by the idea of an evolving consciousness which I derive from the work of Rudolf Steiner. It is commonly assumed that human consciousness has remained essentially the same at least during historical times. Steiner maintained however that there is an evolutionary movement underlying human history, the results of which can be observed. The modern idea of progress assumes a different perspective with a dominant focus on ideas and technical development. The evolution which Steiner speaks of is one of human consciousness. This change is one of potential gain and also of loss. These changes in consciousness are distinguishable from one epoch to the next. A shift of this kind can be observed when we pass from the classical Greek period to the medieval period. A later shift brings us to the modern period. It is especially in philosophy that this phenomenon can be observed.

Plato (427 — 347 BC)

The writings of Plato stand at the beginning of European philosophy. They consist of more than thirty essays or dialogues as they are generally called. Most of them are dialogues in which Socrates, in discussion with other Athenians, examines different philosophical themes such as "justice" and "the good." His method to distinguish truth from falsehood is dialectical; the other participants are necessary for the purpose of the dialogue.

There were other Greeks before Plato, who engaged in philosophy and influenced Plato. Only fragments of their writings remain, but these are also significant for understanding the birth of European philosophy. I shall refer to some of their ideas below.

What is this "philosophy" that begins about the fifth century BC? It is "speculative," meaning it involves a process of mirroring. We can think of it as searching for the ideas that "mirror" the world. For example, we experience "justice" in various ways. But what is it truly? Plato makes use of the dialogue in which Socrates discusses an idea with companions in order to awaken them to think ideas rather than to accept conventions. Socrates would engage in such conversations in the marketplace in Athens or walking with companions in the countryside. He was also a guest in the homes of friends who sought his wisdom. Plato wrote his dialogues many years after the death of Socrates. Only from these dialogues do we know the Socratic method. Plato's teaching was founded on what was taught in the mystery schools. With Plato and his predecessors, a new capacity was being developed. Philosophy is the awakening to the power of thinking. Where did it spring from? There were earlier cultures whose achievements astound us today in Egypt, Iran, India, China, and across the globe. The wisdom to be found in many earlier cultures seems more a gift from a supersensible region than something acquired by speculation and the experience of separation from the object.

Every ancient culture has its mythology. They may share common features but also assume quite distinct aspects which reflect their individual experience. Compare the *Bhagavad Gita* from India with the *Elder Edda* of the Norse people. Their knowledge and wisdom are contained in stories, which are transmitted orally. They speak in pictures, not concepts. In Greece, the mythic stories were the themes of the initiation centers also known as mystery schools. The mythic stories enacted in the mystery schools in Eleusis and in Samothrace were similar yet also quite different from the popular tales of Greek gods and goddesses which we read in childhood. In the works of Plato, we find both the mystery teaching as well as the new dialectical method employed by Socrates.

The institute of the oracle also played a significant part in Greek culture. The most famous was at Delphi on Mount Parnassus. Pythia, a woman inspired by the python (snake), would utter an ecstatic reply to the suppliant's question. This would then be interpreted and rendered in verse.

At this time, Greek was a language, a culture and a people, but Greece was not united in a political state. Each major city and surrounding territory guarded its independent identity jealously. Greek colonies were founded outside Greece in Italy and Asia Minor. Every four years the cities met at Olympia for the sacred games. When the vast Persian Empire attacked the Greeks in 480 BC, the Greeks united and defeated the enemy. After a second attack in which the Persians totally destroyed the city of Athens, Greece was finally liberated. Athens had now to be rebuilt, and out of the ruins a beautiful city was constructed under the leadership of Pericles. The Parthenon, a temple dedicated to the goddess Athene, crowned the Acropolis. The plays of Aeschylus, Sophocles and Euripides were presented in the theatre, and sculpture and painting were developed by artists with a new vision. This was 'the Glory that was Athens" as it was described by enthusiastic scholars of the neineteenth century.

Half a century later, after Athens had reached its height in power and creativity, there followed another disaster. Athens and Sparta had been the chief rivals, and after years of war, Athens was finally defeated. Thucydides, an Athenian who wrote the history of the war between Athens and Sparta, was able to portray these events with a certain objectivity and impartiality. Plato lived through this tempestuous time. When the conflict ended in 404 BC, he was a student of Socrates. The nature of Socrates' method of teaching offended the ruling powers, and he was charged with corrupting the youth and undermining traditional values and beliefs. As a result, he was condemned to death by drinking hemlock. Plato witnessed this event and recounted the last thoughts of his teacher in the dialogue *Phaedo*.

Socrates was the son of a stonemason. He wrote nothing; therefore, what we know of him is mainly derived from Plato's dialogues and the writings of Xenophon. He is described as snub-nosed with the face of a satyr, indifferent to the usual comforts and ambitions. Plato, an aristocrat, inherited the leisure to pursue his own interests. He decided to found an Academy where he could gather students to study philosophy with him. The word itself explains the purpose, philosophia – 'Love of Wisdom." It can also mean 'Wisdom of Love." A knowledge of mathematics was also required of his students.

One of the central dialogues of Plato is titled *Symposium* and has love as its theme. Male friends come together at the home of Agathon to drink wine and be convivial. Socrates arrives late. He had the habit of getting lost in thought, interrupting whatever he was doing. But he eventually turned up. The theme has already been decided on, and after the meal, the pouring of libations and a hymn to the gods, Socrates is invited to speak on love. But there are a number of other lengthy contributions before Socrates begins with a story he heard from a wise woman, Diotima. When Socrates said to her that love is a mighty god and likewise fair, she replied that 'love is neither fair nor good." Socrates retorts, "Then what is not fair must be foul. What is not wisdom must be ignorant." Diotima: 'Not so. In the gap is the mean between wisdom and ignorance, right opinion. Love is neither mortal nor divine; it is in the gap between them" (*Metaxy sofias kai amatheias*).

Diotima

- 13 -

Then Diotima said, "Love is a great spirit (daimon) and like all that is spiritual, love is intermediate between the divine and the mortal." In further discussion, she defines love "as the love of the everlasting possession of the good."

Then she acknowledges, "These definitions belong to the lesser mysteries of love." Now she enters the greater mysteries.

> One begins by loving beauty in one form and having fair thoughts about it. Then one will discover it is related to the beauty in another. Then one recognizes that beauty in every form is one and the same. This may lead to contemplating the beauty of the mind as greater than the beauty of outward things. Further one discovers beauty in laws, institutions and sciences.

> Looking at the abundance of beauty one draws towards the sea of beauty, creating and beholding many fair thoughts in boundless love of wisdom.

> Life that one should live is, above all others, in the contemplation of absolute beauty. Do you not see that in that communion only, beholding beauty with the eyes of the mind, he will be enabled to bring forth, not images of beauty, but realities?

Socrates has described love through the voice of Diotima. She was a priestess of the mysteries, probably of the Eleusinian mystery school, according to Simone Weil. In the dialogues of Plato, we observe the emergence of philosophy from the spirituality that characterized previous cultures.

We live in different times, but if one wants to orient oneself to the world of Plato, then such thoughts can be our guide. The concept of 'the in-between' will surface again in Buber's writings, but in a wholly new setting.

Plato named three predecessors who influenced his philosophy, Pythagoras, Heraclitus, and Parmenides.

Pythagoras lived in the sixth century BC. After traveling widely in the "known" world at that time, he settled in southern Italy where he founded a society to foster his philosophy. Mathematics and music were at the core of his teaching. He is mostly remembered for the theory of right-angled triangles, which bears his name. For Pythagoras the number relationships in musical scales indicated that the cosmos was founded on numbers. Many ideas of the Pythagoreans, such as the Music of the Spheres, are also found in the writings of Plato. Schools of Pythagorean teaching continued for a thousand years.

Heraclitus is believed to have written a book, *On Nature*. As was the custom, he would have deposited this book on the steps of the temple as a dedication to the goddess Artemis in Ephesus. Only fragments of the original now exist. However, there is enough to surmise why the author was important for Plato. Some brief statements are "apophatic," a method for asserting truth by negating or denying certain concepts. This method has been employed in theology as well as in philosophy by several thinkers. One fragment from the book states: "The divine one, whose oracle is in Delphi, speaks neither directly or obscurely, but rather gives a sign."

In this pronouncement, the likely options are rejected and a new approach is indicated.

Hesiod's poem *Theognis* was the traditional account of the Greek myths of creation and the deeds of the Olympian gods and goddesses. Heraclitus wrote, "The One, the only wisdom, does and yet does not consent to be called Zeus." Not a rejection of popular myths but the consent of the Supreme Being is not assured.

The apophatic statement, "I pray to God that I may be free of God", is by Meister Eckhart (1260–1328). On a different theme, a fragment of Heraclitus says: "At night a man kindles a light for himself when his eyes fail to see; thus in life, he is in contact with the dead when asleep and with the sleeper when awake." The following fragment by Heraclitus is also relevant to the philosophy of Plato.

> We acquire understanding by drawing in the Logos through breathing, as we are forgetful when asleep, we regain our senses when we wake up again. For in sleep, when the channels of perception are shut, our mind is shaken loose from its surroundings, and breathing is the only point of contact, to hold on rather like a root; being separated then, our mind loses its former power of memory. But in waking, it again looks out through the channels of perception as through a kind of window, and meeting with the surroundings, it puts on the power of Reason.

Lastly, "We cannot step twice in the same river."

Parmenides maintained that the senses present a world of deception. He writes of the *Way of Truth and the Way of Opinion*. The True is found in what does not perish, and in the unity of everything. In one of Plato's dialogues, the young Socrates is told by Parmenides to learn "the art of thought" from Zeno (a contemporary philosopher).

The *Republic*, also named *Justice*, is one of the longest of Plato's dialogues and one of the most studied. It is divided into ten books. The question it deals with is a simple one: Is it better to be just than unjust?

Two versions of justice are presented. Thrasymachus argues that justice is the interest of the rulers, and Glaucon maintains that justice emerges from an agreement between parties not to harm each other. Socrates then proposes that they look for justice in the community of the city rather than in the individual. As the individual is not self-sufficient, the city is necessary. What does its health consist of? Glaucon comments, "City of pigs! They are all the same." So, at first a "fevered" city suffering from "Inflammation" is considered. A healthy city has become a luxurious city. This leads to the particular needs of such a city to be fulfilled by a particular class. The guardian class will protect the city internally and against enemies outside. It should be gentle to its friends and harsh to its enemies. How should they be educated in order best to fulfill their function?

Initially only two classes are defined – the guardian class to defend the city and the constitution and those who produce the goods – the farmers and the artisans. Later it is realized that without guidance, the city will perish and therefore rulers are needed. The city is threefold – rulers, guardians and producers. The virtue of each class is described. Rulers must have wisdom, guardians must have courage and producers – temperance.

After lengthy discussion led by Socrates, a picture emerges of the just city. Socrates then moves to the ethical question: "What is the just individual?" The virtues required for the just city are now looked for in the just individual. Socrates debates whether the virtues of the three classes in the city are reflected in the threefold nature of the soul. These are described as the "rational soul," the "spirited soul," and the "appetitive soul." The fact that they can be in conflict proves that they are distinctive elements of the soul. As with the three functions in the city, all works well if each part attends to its particular task and cooperates with the other functions without encroaching on them. Socrates asks:

> Is it not then essentially the province of the rational principle to command, inasmuch as it is wise, and has to exercise forethought on behalf of the whole soul and the province of the spirited principle is to be its subject and ally. The third principle, the appetitive soul, is the seat of desires and the other two principles have to be mindful of it.
>
> And so these two, having been thus trained, and having truly learned their parts, and received a real education, will exercise control over the concupiscent principle, which in everyone forms the largest portion of the soul, and is by nature insatiably covetous.

And they watch it narrowly, that it may not so bat-
ten on the pleasures of the body and grow strong to
aspire to dominion over the classes which it has no
right to govern.

Education is essential to bring about the necessary harmony in the
soul. The measures proposed by Socrates impose strong restraints on
group behavior, clear guidance on what is permitted and what is forbidden. Negative influences must be excluded. Popular stories about the gods
and their flirtations must be banned, as the true nature of the divine is
not expressed by them. Much literature and art give untruthful pictures
of the human being and should also be excluded. The warriors, a section
of the guardians, are forbidden to marry and have a family, as that would
interfere with loyalty to the state.

There are a number of other restraints intended to preserve the puri-
ty of the just city. There should be no poverty and wealth should be limited. The first breeds rebels and the second idlers. Rulers should not own
land. Warriors would include women on a basis of equality.

The unresolved question is the intention of Socrates in describing
the just city and the just man. Is he making a detailed plan of a city to be
built? Or is it a utopia (a non-place), an imaginary exercise offered as a
comparison to existing reality? There may be another possibility. Rather
than a prescription for a future city, could it be a set of pertinent questions to awaken the understanding of what justice is. If you want a just
city you need to pay attention to what influences the child, what beliefs
you instill in them, what loyalty you encourage. If you want a just city, you
need rulers who are rational, not rulers driven by their desires or at the
mercy of their spirited soul. If you want a just city, you must be aware of
encouraging unlimited desires.

At the end of Book IX, Socrates makes a statement which is both
illuminating and enigmatic. He is debating with Glaucon whether it is
profitable for a man to be unjust, the simple question with which the

dialogue begins. Then the pros and cons are reviewed. Socrates concludes that the just man will be glad to partake of the character he has gained which has made him a better man and to shun what threatens his exalted condition. Glaucon then remarks, 'If that is his chief concern, he will not get involved in politics." Socrates replies, 'No, he certainly will, at least in his own city, if not in his land." Glaucon answered, 'I understand, he will do so in the city whose organization we have just completed, in the region of speculation, for I don't believe it to be found anywhere on earth." To this Socrates answers: 'Well, perhaps in heaven there is laid up a pattern of it for him who wishes to behold it, and beholding, to organize himself accordingly. And the question of its present or future existence on earth is quite unimportant."

At the beginning of Book VII, Socrates compares our natural condition, so far as education and ignorance are concerned, to a state of affairs described in the Cave of which the following is a summary.

> Imagine the existence of a cave where prisoners have lived since childhood. With their legs and necks so shackled, they have to sit still and look forward; they can see only the shadows that are projected on the wall. Behind the prisoners, a fire burns, and there is a rampart, along which men walk carrying images and all kinds of materials. These cast shadows on the front wall. The prisoners are unable to see the real objects behind them. What the prisoners see and hear are shadows and echoes projected by these objects. These shadows are the only knowledge that the prisoners have about the world. Then, one of the prisoners is freed. Walking through the cave, he realizes that there were people and a fire casting the shadows that he believed to be reality. When he finds his way out of the cave, he is startled when faced with the

outside world. Sunlight obscures his vision, and he feels helpless, uncomfortable, out of place. Gradually, his vision gets used to the light. Then he begins to realize the infinity of the world and nature that exists outside the cave. He realizes that those shadows, which he believed to be reality, are actually imperfect copies of a small portion of reality. The freed prisoner could do two things: return to the cave and free his companions, or depart from the cave to live freely. A possible consequence of the first possibility would be the attacks he would suffer from his companions. If he returns after exposure to sunlight, the dark will obscure his vision. Plato infers that the other prisoners would think that leaving the cave caused blindness and would aggressively oppose an attempt to set them free.

This allegory illustrates what is known in Plato's philosophy as the "Theory of Forms." "Theoria" in ancient Greek meant "contemplation," and "form" was expressed in Plato's writings by "idea" or "eidos" and never meant our modern "idea," meaning "concept." A difficulty in grasping the meaning of Plato's "form" with our contemporary consciousness is that it belongs to a reality outside normal human experience and yet accessible to the mind. In the Symposium, Diotima describes to Socrates the method for experiencing the Form of Beauty, and in the Republic, the Form of Justice is distinguished from opinions about it. Those in the Cave who are only able to see the shadow world are confined to the world of appearances. Those who have been able to leave the Cave and turn to the light know the true world.

The word for truth in Greek is "aletheia." It is composed of a - and lethe. Heidegger, who gave much thought to its meaning, translated "aletheia" as "unconcealment." Lethe is the name of a river in the underworld.

All who drank its waters on returning to this world must forget all memories of life in the other world. If "lethe" means forgetting, "a-letheia" may indicate the "unforgotten" rather than the "unconcealed." Some commentators prefer the former interpretation. In the dialogue Meno, Socrates demonstrates that learning is a process of remembering. That could mean that learning is overcoming the effects of "lethe" and that knowledge is hidden awaiting to be recovered.

For Plato, philosophy was never just an intellectual exercise. In the allegory of the cave, he writes:

> In the world of the knowable, the idea of the Good comes last of all and can be seen with great difficulty, but once it has been seen, it is recognized to be the cause of all that is right and beautiful, because within the world of the visible it generates light.

Aristotle (384 — 322 BC)

No other student in Plato's Academy can compare with Aristotle. It is as if the Academy was created just for him even though it lasted until the sixth century AD when the Byzantine emperor Justinian closed it down. Aristotle spent twenty years in the Academy and only left when Plato died.

He was born in Stagirus (later Stagira) in northeast Greece in the region of Samothrace. Plato's influence on Aristotle was profound and lasted a lifetime. Aristotle also had a pupil, the young Alexander the Great, son of the ambitious Philip, King of Macedon. This relationship had significant consequences in the future. Macedon lay to the north and separate from the Greek city states. It was strongly influenced by Greek culture. Philip and his wife, Olympias, were initiated in the mystery center of Samothrace. When Alexander (356–323 BC) was thirteen, Philip, realizing his exceptional son needed an exceptional tutor, asked Aristotle to take on the task which lasted three years, the relationship continuing until Alexander's death in 323 BC. Aristotle was appointed head of the Royal Academy of Macedon, and, as further reward, Philip rebuilt Stagira, which had recently been completely destroyed in war. This close relation with Macedon was later to damage Aristotle's reputation with the Athenians, whose democracy was being destroyed by these foreigners from the north. Philip succeeded in dominating the Greek city states and planned to set out to conquer Persia and acquire its riches. His murder in 336 BC left the task to his son. Alexander was twenty when he marched his army into Persia. In thirteen years, all the lands from the Mediterranean and Egypt to India fell to his invincible sword. He was a founder of a number of cities, some of which, like Alexandria in Egypt, became important centers for Greek culture. On learning that his teacher, Aristotle, had published certain works, Alexander insisted on receiving copies. Their friendship resulted in the preservation of Aristotle's work in these regions, which later fertilized Islamic civilization.

Alexander had advanced views on cultural differences. He shocked his Greek soldiers, accustomed to consider themselves superior, by wearing Persian garments and, when he had defeated the King of Persia, by marrying his daughter. There are contradictory sides to his character, but these included ideas beyond his time.

On the death of Plato in 347 BC, Aristotle left Athens and traveled in Asia Minor. During his travels, Aristotle stayed in the city of Assos, part of the Persian Empire. In Assos he married Pythias, daughter of Hermias, the ruling chief of that area who had also been a student at Plato's Academy. Aristotle returned with his wife to Greece and later learned that the Persians had attacked Assos. Pythias' father, who was Greek, was tortured and killed, which had a profound effect on Aristotle. He eventually moved to the island of Lesbos where he spent three years studying marine life and plants. He made geological observations, noting lakes that had dried, deserts subsequently watered by rivers, and signs of former volcanoes. His method in studying the creatures on the seashore was to examine the relation between parts and their functions in the overall harmony of the animal's structure. He was especially impressed by the beauty of these structures. He was able to examine hundreds of specimens and some of his discoveries were only confirmed in the nineteenth century. While he does not appear to have made experiments like a modern biologist his observations were systematic and exacting.

Aristotle then returned to Athens and founded his school, the Lyceum, in rented buildings beside the temple of Apollo Lyceus. Much of the work which we now have may have been delivered as lectures and then transcribed for circulation. It is believed that Aristotle may have written up to two hundred books of which about thirty one have survived.

From the works that survived, we get some idea of the wide range of interests that occupied Aristotle. The works included investigations in Physics, Biology, Zoology, Metaphysics, Logic, Ethics, Aesthetics, Poetry,

Theatre, Music, Rhetoric, Psychology, Linguistics, Economics, Politics, Meteorology, and Government.

If one wishes to study any of these subjects, one cannot do better than begin with Aristotle. His philosophy has influenced European culture like no other, also giving the Catholic Church an understanding of the world, which could support its religious impulse.

Aristotle spent about twenty years studying under his master Plato. He must have fully absorbed the philosophical teachings given in the dialogues, and also given much thought to Plato's "Theory of Forms" as the foundation for understanding reality. He must also have pondered on the world of appearances, on change, growth, development, on causality, on the nature of life, and on all activities, thoughts, and opinions that occupied people outside the Academy. Fragments of dialogues exist which seem to indicate a Platonic stage in his development. By the time he came to establish the Lyceum, however, he seems to have taken a radically new orientation in his philosophy.

The Lyceum was very different from the Academy of Plato. It was more like a research center, which included a library, the first of its kind in Europe. The students read books and studied the literature of other thinkers. Its task was to enhance the thinking so that the students could begin to understand the world around them.

De Anima (On the Soul) can serve as an introduction to Aristotle's philosophy. It is unclear why the title is in Latin; perhaps because the Greek title, "On the Psyche", would be confusing. The book describes the living world of plants, animals and human beings, how they manifest themselves, their functions and "aims." Aristotle's style of writing is very different from Plato's. He assembles his information, cites opinions of writers; he gives credit to the deserving, selects the most important, and establishes a framework of thoughts. He likes to support his ideas with clear everyday similes. He does not usually offer the elegant polished speeches in which Plato conducts the dialogue. Because of his manner of tentatively exploring his thoughts, it is not easy to definitively encapsulate them. Sometimes his writings appear more like a draft being prepared for further development. In Book 1, Chapter 1, of *De Anima* Aristotle explains the task addressed in the book.

> The soul is, so to speak, the first principle of living things. We seek to contemplate and know its nature and substance and then the things that are accidental to it. In general and in all ways, it is one of the hardest of things to gain any conviction about the soul.

Substance literally means "what stands under" and so refers to what underlies the visible world. The world we perceive with our modern eyes has been described as theory-laden. We have the concept for the thing out there almost without observing it. But observations by Aristotle seem to be in search of an appropriate concept. Observation is the prime tool; from it the idea (concept) can then emerge. Do we not so often start with the concept?

After preliminary thoughts on traditional views of the soul in Book 2, the concepts "matter," "potential," and "actual" are explained. When the eye is closed or asleep its capacity to see is "potential," when awake, "actual." Matter is only potential, and only when united with "form," which is actual, is it actualized. Aristotle's "form" is different from Plato's.

> Sleeping and waking are a part of the soul's being present, and waking is like contemplation, sleeping like having but not employing knowledge. And since knowledge is in the individual case prior in origin, soul is the first actuality of a natural body which potentially has life.

While this quote may at first be perplexing for the modern reader, it reveals the mind of Aristotle at work. The above statement applies equally to a primrose, a dog, or a human being. The word "knowledge" seems to refer to the state in which we are able to know and not what has been acquired through knowing. A seed has potentiality for life. Placed in suitable soil, it becomes actual and ensouled. When a human being or animal is asleep, its "knowledge" is potential, when awake, "knowledge" is actual. Aristotle differentiates three kinds of soul life, plant, animal, and human.

> For the moment we may be taken to have made the following claim, that the soul is the principle of these things we have mentioned, and is defined by these things, the nutritive, perceptive, and intellective faculties and movement.

A little later:

> But nothing yet is clear on the subject of the intellect and the contemplative faculty.

This is developed into the following:

> All such beings have a nutritive soul which initiates and guides their most basic functions, the absorption of food, growth, and reproduction of its kind. All animals also have a sensitive soul by means of which they perceive features of their surroundings and move in response to the stimuli they provide. Human beings also possess in addition a rational soul that permits representation and thought.

On this basis Aristotle investigates the three souls, the nutritive, the sensitive, and the rational. He also examines the different senses, sense perception, imagination (which refers to an enhanced level of perception), and the intellect. He explains the intellect which exists in two states, our ordinary intellect linked to perceptions, memories, etc., and the separate intellect which does not sleep.

It is not the case that the intellect is now thinking, now not. It is, further, in its separate state that
the intellect is just that which it is, and it is this alone
that is immortal and eternal, though we have no
memory, as the separate intellect is unaffected, while
the intellect that is affected is perishable, and in any
case thinks nothing without the other.

This appears to come out of the blue as we now learn of two kinds of
thinking: an immortal and a perishable one. The immortal one is always
actualized, while it seems that the mortal intellect can sleep and be potential. In Aristotle's picture of the living world, the functions of nutritive,
perceptive, and rational souls form a hierarchy in which the organisms'
"knowledge" (ability to know) moves from lower to higher. Note that the
concept "know" applies to plants as well as animals. Flowers turn to the
sun, tree roots communicate.

In Aristotle's *Ethics,* the central theme is the nature of "happiness" (eudaimonia), which Aristotle characterizes as having three
different possibilities:

1. The slavish way of pleasure, which is the way the
   majority of people think of happiness.
2. The aristocrat and man of affairs identify the good
   with honor, which may fairly be described as the
   end pursued in political and public life.
3. The way of contemplation.

According to Aristotle, the best approach in studying controversial
subjects like ethics or politics, which involve such themes as what is beautiful or just, is to start from what would be agreed by the educated and those
with life experience, and then work from there to a higher understanding.

The proverb says that "the half is greater than
the whole," but we may go further and say that the

beginning is greater than the whole, for the beginning clears up many obscurities together in the matter we may be investigating.

So far, we have merely drawn the outline of happiness; the details must be filled in gradually. In the exact sciences, precise conclusions are needed and reached once for all. In ethics, we can only approximate to such conclusions.

Is happiness capable of being acquired by some intellectual process or the formation of a habit or does it come to us by some divine inspiration, or even the caprice of events? It is the direction of the soul's energies on sound moral principles that makes us happy, their direction towards evil that makes us unhappy.

Aristotle then relates virtues like courage and generosity to happiness. Moral virtues we acquire by first exercising them, like the arts and crafts. Then they become a habit.

So, it is a matter of real importance whether our early education confirms us in one set of habits or another. It would be nearer the truth to say it makes a very great difference indeed, in fact all the difference in the world.

Virtues are destroyed by deficiency and by excess. Someone who runs away is a coward, while someone who fears nothing is rash. In this way the virtue "courage" can be seen as being a "mean" between two extremes. Instead of prescribing virtues to be followed, Aristotle adopts an artistic approach. One might compare it to a Greek sculpture by Praxiteles where a figure stands upright on one foot with the other foot raised. This potential state of unbalance is counterbalanced by an appropriate response on the upper side in the shoulder and arm. This was achieved by the Greek genius and failed by their Roman imitators who required metal supports. This same artistic approach is revealed in the way Aristotle describes the virtues. One has to intuit the point of balance.

Here is a selection of virtues giving the true virtue or mean in the center with the deficient and the excessive on either side.

Deficient	Virtue/ Mean	Excessive
Cowardice	Courage	Rashness
Miserliness	Liberality	Prodigality
Abstinence	Temperance	Drunkenness
Self-deprecation	Truthfulness	Boastfulness
Pettiness	Magnificence	Vulgarity

Aristotle explains and gives examples of each virtue together with its deficient and its excessive form. He goes on to point out that it is not easy to achieve the mean, the place of balance between the excesses on either side. Aristotle wrote:

> Anyone can get angry, and easily, and give and spend money; but to do this to the right person, to the right extent, at the right time, with the right purpose and in the right manner, is not something that anyone can do, nor is it easy; that is why good conduct is rare and praiseworthy and noble.

In these brief extracts from *De Anima* and *The Ethics,* we get to know some aspects of Aristotle's way of working. We can now approach our primary task of examining Aristotle's theory of knowledge and then comparing it to that of Plato.

In order to proceed we must first become familiar with certain concepts and their meaning for Aristotle: Logic, Causality, Teleology, and Theory of Forms.

1. Logic

Aristotle's work on logic constitutes a major contribution to philosophy. Although previous thinkers were aware of the need to be logical in argument, it was Aristotle who made logic into a science which could provide guidance in the thought process. The syllogism is an example of logical inference.

All men are mortal.

Socrates was a man.

Therefore, Socrates was mortal.

If the first two sentences or propositions are true, then the third must also be true.

If A=C and A=B then C=B. This logical connection implies an inevitable conclusion.

Aristotle's logic became an enduring discipline in European philosophy right up until the nineteenth century. It provided a deductive system to show that propositions derived from indubitable axioms can be proven to be true. Aristotle also defined the proposition or judgement as follows: A proposition is a sentence with a subject and a predicate. It can be based on observation, on deduction (e.g., Pythagoras' theorem) or induction (e.g., the earth moves round the sun). Philosophy's task is to test the truth and validity of propositions.

2. Causality

Aristotle distinguishes four levels of causality. In the case of a bronze statue, we can identify:

Material cause: What is it made of? Bronze.

Formal cause: What is its form, its organization? A statue.

Efficient cause: What brings it about? The sculptor.

Final cause: What is the end to which it moves? The created work.

Each cause poses a question to which the answer is not predetermined. This is Aristotle's method of studying processes which go on in nature, in the crafts, in government, and in all aspects of life. His manner of joining together processes which at first seem unconnected generates a sense of unity and wholeness.

3. Teleology

The final cause or "moving towards completion," Aristotle calls "entelechy." When Aristotle states that "happiness" is the end of human action, he means that our actions should be governed by what will bring about that end and these should be virtuous. However, there are many examples of virtuous individuals who came to an unhappy end, like Socrates. For Aristotle, God is the original cause of a changing universe, but he does not state an end (telos). Traditional Christianity speaks of an end and of "virtues" to attain it. Modern scientists reject attempts to import any sign of teleology into science. Edourd Zeller, a German writer in the 1808 reassured his contemporaries that Aristotle was not the wrong kind of teleologist. "The most important feature of the Aristotelian teleology is the fact that it is neither anthropocentric nor is it due to the actions of a creator existing outside."

4. Theory of Forms

This is central to Plato's philosophy. For Plato, the forms or "Ideas" exist only in the eternal world of spirit. They are real, true, and timeless and accessible to man by contemplative research. In the physical world appear transient imitations which are separate from the real archetypes.

Aristotle claimed that the "form" is immanent in the physical object. It is the organizing principle in plants, animals, and humans and in each organ.

One might sum up *The Ethics* as laying the foundations for Aristotle's theory of knowledge, that is, understanding what it means to know. It also provides us with a framework that may illuminate much of what follows in later chapters.

The first task is to understand what Aristotle means by "essence" or "basic truth." Quadruped relates to dog as a higher truth. Animal represents a higher truth to quadruped, and living creature represents a further higher truth. Thus, one arrives at the "essence" or "basic truth." The following argument will elucidate Aristotle's view.

"Living things have a nutritive soul" is a proposition of Aristotle. The subject "living things" is a truth which is deduced from a higher truth and linked to the predicate, "have a nutritive soul." This results from an inductive (at least partly) process of observation and discovery. If the subject, "living things" has no higher truth, then it is the essence or "basic truth." For example, a higher truth to "living things" might be "existent on earth." Genus is a higher truth to species.

The "basic truth" that cannot be deduced is foundational. Aristotle concludes that the object of this knowledge is the universal form which is also Plato's objective.

Plato and Aristotle are often compared to each other, Aristotle being portrayed as fundamentally opposed to the Platonic world. Indeed, there are many examples to show that they differ on important issues.

I found the following excerpt from an essay published by Loyola University and unattributed. It is a clear presentation of Aristotle's epistemology, showing where they differ and in what way they share similar understanding of mind. It offers, I believe, a credible insight into the question.

> Let us examine how we know a dog named Fido. Aristotle agrees with Plato that knowledge is of what is true, and that this truth must be justified in a way that shows it must be true, it is necessarily true. Since physical particulars, the beings or substances of which reality is made can change, the object of knowledge cannot be the particular, but must be of that which is "universal." When I know "Fido is a dog," I know by sensory observation a sensory, perishable, individual object, the dog "Fido." But in knowing he is a dog, what I know, the object of my knowledge, is the universal "dogness" found not only in Fido but in

millions of other substances, it is the "commensurate universal," that which all the particulars exhibiting a form have in common. In this, Aristotle and Plato are in agreement that the object of knowledge is the universal form or, as it came to be known, "essence" or "essential nature." However, the Aristotelian form differs from the Platonic in that it is in the substance, (in rem, in Latin, as opposed to the Platonic ante rem, signifying Plato's view that the form's existence is independent of the physical particulars) and there is nothing "other worldly" about the object of knowledge for Aristotle.

Furthermore, unlike in Plato, in Aristotle there is no putting down of sensory perception as a hindrance to knowledge in order to elevate the mental. I become acquainted with the form in the substance directly; I see the dogness in Fido. Thus, it is through the senses that we begin to gain knowledge of the form which makes the substance the particular substance it is. But while the process begins with sensory perception, genuine "knowledge" is not delivered simply in the act of perception, but rather attained only in the "judgment" that what I perceive has this particular form. From the memory records of repeated perceptions, Aristotle tells us "experience" is born. (Note that this Aristotelian definition of "experience" as requiring the mind's ability to somehow find what is common in the mind's records is altogether different from the way the same word is used in Enlightenment philosophy, which opposes what we know by "experience" to that which we know by the mind.) The "organ" that apprehends

> the universal in experience is not the senses but nous,
> that is, the mind or rational intuition which is "given
> directly" to the mind.

In other words, the widely held view that Aristotle rejected the teaching of Plato needs to be re-examined.

The fresco known as *The School of Athens*, painted by Raphael, depicts Plato and Aristotle walking forward against a blue sky and under imposing arches amid some forty famous Greeks. Plato gestures upwards and Aristotle holds the palm of his right hand at the level of the heart and horizontal with the earth. Plato carries the dialogue *Timaeus* and Aristotle the *Ethics*. They do not seem to move in different worlds but rather to acknowledge their tasks in developing philosophies which, in spite of important differences, are complementary rather than oppositional.

Plato expresses views that refer us to the past. The soul pre-exists this life and knowledge is a reminiscence from this former life. Both these ideas are rejected by Aristotle. He looks forward. For him knowledge arises out of present research in a world always moving towards future ends, a teleological world.

This final thought of Aristotle points again to thinking's split nature, ordinary and separate thinking.

> Thought by itself cannot be the supreme
> good because one can think of the worst thoughts.
> Therefore, the divine thought thinks itself, it is what
> is best, and its thinking is a thinking of thinking.

Augustine of Hippo (354 — 430 AD)

Human consciousness is usually considered to be constant. The world and the way human beings perceive it have not changed but the understanding of it has. In earlier cultures this has been limited and usually false. Experience, the discovery of different substances like metals, the cultivation of grains, and the invention of new tools from blow pipes to wind mills and steamengines have enabled human populations to emerge from ignorance. However, this view can be seen as a modern fantasy. Humanity in its long history has emerged from a relationship to the universe very different from that of the modern self-conscious, self-centered, on-looking, introspective individual. Its consciousness could be described as that of a dream. It was a dreaming which, however, was also a kind of knowing. Relationship to plants, animals, and the natural elements existed out of an instinctive consciousness. As people became more conscious of their individuality, their instinctive knowledge became dimmed. Wise shamans and rishis were the guides of the people. In the civilizations which preceded that of the Greeks, in India, Persia, Babylonia, and Egypt, pharaohs and god-kings were looked up to as being possessed by the god. This kind of rulership was in decline when Greek philosophy undertook the intellectual task of conscious search for knowledge and wisdom. Human consciousness had reached the stage when this became a necessity. In the philosophy of the next period or epoch which follows the advent of the Christian revelation, the works of Augustine will be our study.

Since the time of Aristotle and the conquests of Alexander the Great, the world has changed dramatically. Rome had become the ruler over most of southern and western Europe as well as much of North Africa and the Middle East.

The concept of the citizen, "civis," is an important creation of Roman culture. By the time of the founding of the Roman Empire under the emperor Augustus in 27 BC, an individual from any part of the empire could acquire Roman citizenship and Latin, the Roman language, was not obligatory. Religions and beliefs once firmly linked to a particular culture now either spread or lost their hold. Jewish thought mingled with Greek; the Egyptian Isis was worshiped in Rome. The events out of which Christianity began and which changed the culture of Europe were hardly noticed by contemporary historians.

The destruction of the Temple in Jerusalem by the Romans in 70 AD was to quell rebellious Jews, not to repress a religion, and was a small incident in the story of a mighty empire. However, the aftermath of these events was monumental, extending its influence on Europe and the world even into our times. The view that religions and spiritual movements are more or less cultural impositions by dominant groups whose irrational beliefs were designed to keep the down-trodden in subjection and the rulers in power, is commonly held today. Such a view fails to grasp the significance of Christianity which permeated the minds and lives of all the peoples inhabiting Europe until the nineteenth century. For centuries, art, architecture, music, all branches of literature were inspired by it. Many of the men and women we honor today were imbued by the spirit of Christianity. The decline of its institutions is a significant issue but does not annihilate the human spirit. To understand Augustine, one has to enter into his search for a new foundation for society and human well-being. Dante, Leonardo, Raphael, Shakespeare, Newton, and Beethoven and the majority of Europe's leading figures until the nineteenth century have been influenced by the same source as Augustine.

It was in the Age of Enlightenment (the eighteenth century) that a shift in interest brought about a rejection of beliefs and attitudes that earlier centuries had assumed as God-given. This age had its roots in the Renaissance and the scientific investigations of Galileo and others. A new scientific truth began to replace an older one of "Man made in the image of God." We have to be especially attentive when we read Augustine by not imposing our attitudes on a journey we are not taking. The events recorded in the New Testament were historical facts for Augustine. For him these historical events were not viewed in the manner of a present-day historian, as a record of events for academic study. The events of Golgotha, the crucifixion and resurrection of Christ had changed the world, and Augustine knew it was his task to make the world aware of the depth of that change.

Augustine was born and raised in Tagaste in North Africa, not far from ancient Carthage. The Carthaginians had been the great enemies of Rome, and their city was destroyed by the Romans in the second century BC, before being rebuilt. Augustine spoke the old Carthaginian language. His mother was Christian, and his father was pagan. He was ambitious, full of energy, sociable, made many friends, and as a sixteen-year-old, he already had a mistress. He studied at the University of Carthage, learning the art of rhetoric, which was important in those days. If one hoped to be a senator or be part of any public organization, one had to speak well and know how to convince one's audience. It was his intention to become a teacher of rhetoric.

However, at the age of twenty, Augustine became dissatisfied with his life. He began to look around, questioning what it all meant. He encountered people who were Manichaeans (followers of Mani who lived a hundred years before in Persia) whose teachings included elements of Christianity. Augustine was part of this movement for about ten years. However, he became dissatisfied with it to the extent that he later became a vociferous opponent of the movement. Our knowledge of Manichaeism has come largely from descriptions by its enemies. Revelations in the twentieth century have shown that there was actually a great deal more in Manichaeism than Augustine was familiar with.

In his early thirties, he crossed over to Italy where he encountered the remarkable teacher Ambrose of Milan (340–397 AD) and as a result became a Christian. His mother, of course, was delighted that her son had finally entered the fold.

Augustine's *Confessions* is the book which, of all his works, is still published in popular editions. It is a description of his early life and memories. He describes how the child learns, how memory awakens and explores the chamber of the mind, the nature of sense perception, forgetfulness, thinking, and truth and error. He makes a study of his own inner life with amazing clarity. This is effectively the first autobiography by a European. No one had thought that telling your own story could be of any importance. Plutarch (46–119 AD), who wrote about the lives of famous people, began his biographies when the subjects were aged about sixteen. At that age they could hold responsible positions and fight in battles. For Plutarch, the child was a product of his ancestry and that was sufficient to define him. Augustine, on the other hand, reflecting on his childhood, wonders why he is even resisting his mother in the cradle. 'Why do I do that? Why is this quality that lives in the human soul so antipathetic to goodness? Right from birth, we are like this. Why?' He goes on to relate that at the age of eleven, he was with some friends, when they decided to leap over a wall and steal some pears from an orchard. They don't want the pears because they're all well fed so they throw them away. He then reflects, 'Why did I do that?' He reflects on his life and sees himself through a new lens that he has discovered in his faith. He looks at his early life in this critical way, not just acknowledging what happened but wondering: 'What's the source of this? Why does it come about that human beings act like this?' Then he ponders on his whole adventure with the Manicheans. 'What was happening with me there? Why was I drawn into that?' Such is the substance of his autobiography *Confessions*.

It is difficult for us to recognize ourselves in a Cicero or a Pericles from the accounts given. But when we read Augustine, who lived in a unique time and place, his story resonates with us. We can understand why he is called Prophet of the Personality.

He writes about the abyss of human consciousness. (There's no similar abyss in Plato or Aristotle.) Augustine assumes the task of investigating and penetrating the nature of the abyss, the abyss of personality.

Augustine's *Confessions* is divided into thirteen short books. The last four are usually omitted from popular editions. Fortunately, I was allowed to use the library in a nearby monastery, which I did several times. No other reader was ever there. An alcove of shelves contained the entire writings of Augustine in Latin and English. I copied Book 10 and will quote some of the contents. In it Augustine transitions from autobiography to a more direct exploration of philosophical and theological questions of human existence. There he confronts the abyss which has to do with self-love. He has traveled through a wilderness of self-love and intellectual arrogance and he has arrived home. He asks, "What is this love of the divine that I experience? What is it that I love when I love the divine? How do I go beyond the power I share with animals, that ties me to my body and fills the whole of it with life?"

Although not framed in a contemporary language, Augustine has arrived at the realization that answers to his questions lie entirely within, a very contemporary realization. In his search for an answer to his question, he reflects on the nature of memory. The following are paraphrases and excerpts from Book 10 of the *Confessions*. They are drawn from several pages and need to be read in toto to be properly appreciated and give us an insight into the qualities of Augustine's thinking.

> I enter the many chambers of memory.
> Countless images appear imported by the senses.
> What I demand appears immediately or later.
> Images I don't want I dismiss with the hand of
> my heart from the face of my remembrance.
> Images follow each other in order as they are
> suggested.

He goes on to reflect on the character of the images:

Images are set out under general headings, color, shape, plant, etc.

Things themselves don't enter the storeroom, only images.

Who knows how they are made?

In darkness and silence, I make appear color and sounds.

In the vast memory chamber distant things are near – stars, Rome.

I meet myself, remembering what I have done and how I felt.

And on consciousness more generally, he states:

I will to do this or that, hope for this or that, and images appear.

Who has grasped the depth of this chamber?

It belongs to me, yet I do not grasp all of it.

Where is that part I do not grasp?

Outside of me and not in myself?

How then does it not grasp itself?

Admiration and astonishment seize me!

When I learned things like Pythagoras' theorem, I perceived them in my own way, not just believing the teacher.

When we learn not by the senses but see within us what they are themselves, without images, what are they?

Joy and sadness can be remembered without being joyful or sad.

Privation of memory is forgetfulness.

How can that be present for me to remember, since when it is so I cannot remember?

How can I say that I remember forgetfulness?

This wonderful power of memory does not

reach to the divine.

From these excerpts we can learn to appreciate a certain quality of thinking. Augustine proposes: "When I seek the divine, I seek a happy life." Then he asks: "Where did I acquire this notion so that I can search for it?"

It was important for Augustine to bring certainty to his Christian faith. For Aristotle, knowledge of the truth had to be certain to be acceptable and this required recognition of first principles. Knowledge of the world requires observation of separate things and assembling these into groups, which are then seen to belong to higher groups. The particular horse I see belongs to a group, which is contained in the higher group animal, which belongs to the living. In this way, one arrives at first principles. Augustine also recognized the need for such certainty however. Because of man's insufficiency, he reaches for something greater than himself. Knowledge of that which is greater is essential for his happiness. How does the finite mind which changes, attain certainty of truths? For truth then rules the mind and so transcends it. Anticipating Descartes, Augustine concludes, "If one doubts one knows, one knows one exists" (Si fallor sum).

In his demand for certainty, it was clear to Augustine that the central revelation of Christianity could not be established by reason. The existence of God might be proved by reason, but that was not sufficient to align the human will with the will of God, as he knew from personal experience. Faith for Augustine was not a poor substitute for knowledge. It is a force in its own right. He writes: "I believe that I may understand" (Credo ut intelligam). As well as faith, there is also grace, a divine gift needed for the human being to be saved. Reason can awaken the individual to faith, and then he can undertake the exploration of faith, its grounds and its consequences. Augustine is fundamentally concerned with the existential situation, with what it means to be living in the world, a world that is falling apart.

Rome was sacked by Gothic tribes in 410 AD. Franks, Vandals and other tribes penetrated the broken empire from the northeast and eventually settled in western and southern regions of Europe. The Vandals (who have given their name to the English language because of their ferocity and the fear they inspired) passed through France and Spain, then crossed to North Africa and arrived at the gates of Hippo, where Bishop Augustine lay dying. The year was 430 AD.

Augustine's writings are voluminous. His major work *The City of God* took thirteen years to write. It bears comparison with Plato's *Republic,* which was about the question of justice in a community. Plato's philosophy deals with the understanding and attainment of the Good. In contrast, Augustine is concerned with existence and the relationship to God. God is a being with whom man can relate. He traces the revelation of this being through the Old Testament and the writings of the Greek philosophers. For Augustine, "The City of God" is not an already existing state but it emerges in history.

In order to show that a spiritual idea can be grounded, he chooses the example of the Trinity. The trinity is all around us, he explains. He shows how reason probes the area of Revelation. All questions, for example, can be assigned to three different areas, the natural world – the rational world and the moral world.

1. Physical questions: the weather: food, health, sailing of ships, etc.
2. Rational questions: truth, beauty: art and music, mathematics, etc.
3. Moral questions: forgiveness: duty, good and evil, love your enemy.

There is also a trinity in being an artist. One has to practice; one needs skills and also innate qualities. One cannot be a painter without painting. One needs skills, which develop with practice. The artist also needs an innate quality essential for his work.

Reflecting in this way he offers an approach to the image of the Trinity.

The City of God is Augustine's most influential work. In the debates between Catholics and Protestants in the seventeenth century, this book was consulted for guidance by both sides. In it, Augustine describes the two cities: the Earthly and the Heavenly, which represent two attitudes of mind, two types of people who have opposed sets of social values. The first is holy, the second foul; the first is social, the second selfish; the first consults the common good for the sake of a celestial society, the second grasps at a selfish control of social affairs for the sake of arrogant domination; the first is submissive to God, the second seeks to rival God; the first is quiet, the second restless, etc.

The lessons offered by Augustine need to be understood in the following light. People at that time lived in a society where tribal traditions determined behavior. All power came from above, from the chief and the demands of the gods. Only the individual capable of internalizing his experience could challenge these traditions. The importance of Augustine's teaching lay in its fostering of this process. It gives emphasis to an individual sense of responsibility, which goes beyond tribal allegiance. It lays a basis for later epochs when freedom is the cry.

Augustine's conception of love differs from that of the Greeks and the modern experience of personal love for another. Socrates visits Diotima of Mantinea in his search for the nature of love. She teaches that love arises in the in-between, between human and the divine, between beauty and ugliness. It is an inner force that transforms. For Aristotle, love is something quite other. Love searches for perfection. It is there in the plant, which loves to perfect itself, to come into blossoming and into fruiting. Love is like a diversified force in the universe, the universe that moves towards perfection.

For Augustine, it is love of the divine, which he seeks. It is no abstract notion but a lived experience. The divine is not an otherworldly reality but a presence in this world. Love has attended on humanity since its beginning; it is not an invention at some stage. Like all manifestations of human consciousness, it has its trajectory and unfolding. Augustine makes love an intimate experience that takes one beyond the soul but yet within reach of the soul.

In *The City of God* Augustine draws our attention to the question of human freedom, a concept which was not formulated by the thinkers of classical Greece and Rome: "What universal way of freeing the souls is there but that which frees all souls, and consequently without which none is freed."

Thomas Aquinas (1225 — 1274)

The teaching of Augustine was to deepen the inner life and strengthen the sense of personal responsibility for one's actions. Augustine was also concerned with finding a basis of certainty for Christian faith. Another theme which concerned him and would preoccupy Christians right up to the seventeenth century was the question of predestination. Put simply, it asserts that salvation is predestined before birth and does not finally depend on individual striving. This would seem to be in opposition to Augustine's concept of free will. How, therefore, could he defend predestination? Pelagius (354–418), a theologian from the islands of Britain, openly opposed the idea of predestination, contending that every soul comes onto the Earth and has to work through his own destiny out of his own capacities for salvation. However, Augustine was obliged to defend predestination and was supported by his great contemporary Jerome. St Jerome (c. 342/47–420) was responsible for the translation of the Old and the New Testaments into Latin which remained the official translation in the Catholic Church until the twentieth century.

The question of predestination was a burning issue at the time, and Augustine devoted volumes to the condemnation of Pelagius' notion of free will. Imagine the situation: The Roman Empire is collapsing, Jerome is living in Bethlehem, Augustine in North Africa, and Pelagius is elsewhere in the Middle East, and the three of them engaged in intensive debate with each other. When Augustine and Jerome brought the teaching of Pelagius to a church council in 416 AD it was condemned, and Pelagius excluded from the Catholic communion. Steiner comments on the background to this debate: "You'll notice if you look back into the past, originally, there was no such thing as individual salvation. For the Hebrews, it was always taught that a people had to be saved, not the individual." The contest between these two medieval scholars is over the question of free will, which is still debated today.

About seven hundred years separate the lives of Augustine and Aquinas. A brief overview of some key milestones will help us make the transition to the time of Aquinas. Christianity had already been established as the official religion of the Roman Empire by Emperor Constantine in 323 AD. As Roman rule in the West disintegrated the invasions of various tribes, including the Goths, Vandals, Lombards, Avars, and Huns brought chaos and destruction. This period when tribal chiefs fought for territory and supremacy over other tribes is known as the Dark Ages.

There was, however, an important source of illumination during that time of conflict in Europe, and that was centered in Ireland. Thomas Cahill in *How the Irish Saved Civilization* has maintained just that, and that Europe was saved by the skin of its teeth by the Irish. Among these Celtic monks were Columba of Iona, Aidan of Lindisfarne, St Gaul, and St Cuthbert who, independent from the influence of Rome, brought Christianity to the eastern and northern parts of the British Isles. On the small island of Skellig Michael off the southeast coast of Ireland, we can glimpse today what kind of conditions these monks lived in. The access across rough seas is difficult in winter. A steep rocky path amid nesting seabirds arrives at a peak where the monastery and living quarters were constructed. Dwellings shaped like beehives were of uncut stone and only the small church was weatherproof. This monastic culture created artistic wonders like *The Book of Kells*. These Irish monks not only preserved but also evolved a concept of Christianity different from that of Rome, which then spread out into Europe, to places like St. Gallen in Switzerland.

On Christmas day 800 AD, Charlemagne, King of the Franks, was crowned Holy Roman Emperor by the Pope in Rome. The capital of the empire was at Aachen in present-day Germany. While this was to bring a certain stability to Western Europe, Christendom was now threatened by a new danger. The invading army of Islam, having crossed the narrow straits of Gibraltar from Africa to Spain, threatened the Frankish kingdom. The grandfather of Charlemagne, Charles Martel, had defeated the Muslims at Tours in 732, but the conflict with Islam as a military and ideological opponent was just beginning. When the Turkish armies of

Islam conquered Palestine and the holy city of Jerusalem, the Pope in 1095 aroused Christian reaction and the determination to recover the land which witnessed the events at the foundation of their belief. The first Crusade captured Jerusalem, and it was held for a hundred years and then lost. The endeavors to recapture the Holy Land continued for centuries and ended when Islam spread into southeastern Europe with its conquest of Byzantium.

It is appropriate to write a paragraph about the Troubadours, poets who wrote and sang in the dialect of southern France, Provencal or Langue d'oc. They flourished in the twelfth and thirteenth centuries and exercised an extraordinary influence on the culture of that time. Kings and princes, court life and society were affected by their literary output. Their theme was love. The love between two people expressed in idealistic language is not to be found in earlier European culture. Italian poets like Dante and Petrarch belonged to the movement. In its deepest sense it inaugurated a freeing of the personality from the bonds of family, blood, and communal obedience. Shakespeare's *Romeo and Juliet* developed from the Troubadour theme.

Thomas Aquinas was born in Italy in 1225. His parents were of the nobility and related to emperors, kings, and princes. At the age of five, he was already learning from the Benedictines who were close by at Monte Casino. He was a brilliant child, destined by inclination for monastic life, in spite of the opposition of his family, especially his mother. At that time, there were two religious orders that had come into being to renew the Christian life: the Dominican Order, inspired by the Spaniard St Dominic, and the Franciscan Order, inspired by St Francis of Assisi. These orders had the blessing of the Pope, and their influence spread throughout Europe. They differed from what was already established in the Benedictine and Augustine Orders. The Franciscan Order embodied the principles of St Francis who had the strong impulse to work with the poor and the disadvantaged. By contrast, St Dominic had the impulse to impart the knowledge and beliefs of the Church, hence his order is a teaching order. When he was still an adolescent, Aquinas decided to join the Dominicans. His parents thought these new orders of monks were beneath the level of their culture, preferring the Benedictines. The resistance was so strong that he was captured and imprisoned by his brothers in order to prevent him becoming a Dominican. However, after two years of persistence, he eventually got his way. At that time, universities were being founded in Padua, Paris and then later, in Oxford. After studying for two years in Cologne under the Dominican Albertus Magnus, who was himself one of the greatest philosopher/theologians of the Middle Ages, Aquinas went on to become a Doctor of Theology at the University of Paris.

Aquinas and Albertus are the supreme representatives of the Scholastic period. The Catholic Church is at the summit of its power in Western Europe. The Gothic style of architecture expresses confidence in its mission and a new dedication to its spiritual tasks. It is a time when new questions are raised about the nature of faith and reason. The *Summa Theologica*, written in the last nine years of Aquinas' life, presents his thoughts on God, Humanity, its relation to the Divine and to its earthly tasks, and finally the individual response to Christ. It is devoted entirely to religious issues and from today's perspective, it might be argued, has no place in philosophical studies. Nevertheless, the scholastics, of whom Aquinas was arguably the greatest, were also preoccupied with problems of the nature of thinking and of the individual's power to establish truths that have certainty. These issues have already appeared in Augustine's thinking, but now they are studied intensely as philosophical questions. Lying behind the *Summa* is a thorough epistemology and study of thinking.

We can now review the difference in the nature of ideas as experienced by Plato and by the scholastic thinkers. Let us consider Plato's metaphor of the Cave. According to this allegory, we are only seeing shadows in our everyday experience of the world. We remain chained to this view until we break the chain and turn around to experience reality in the light of the sun. For Plato, the world of Ideas is the only reality. But this view no longer fitted the experience of the scholastics. For them, Ideas were real, underlying the visible world and grasped by the intellect. This position was termed Realism, and the philosophical task was to validate Ideas through thinking. Deductive thinking, drawing conclusions from what is known by reason and logic: that is the method of the scholastics. A challenge to this view had already appeared in the eleventh century, termed Nominalism, which maintained that Ideas, or "universals" as they were then called, had no reality. According to the nominalists, the world consists of particular objects and events, and universals are just labels we attach to such objects. Aquinas defended the Realist position. For him, nominalists were abandoning an essential element which supports our understanding of the world. If only particulars are real and there is no reality in ideas which unite particulars, then the basis for knowledge is threatened. Then the Trinity which unites Father, Son, and Holy Spirit can have no reality or meaning. In the following centuries, Nominalism would flourish and the Realist view was rejected and no longer understood.

After the death of Aristotle, his books were more or less lost. The person he had bequeathed them to, Theophrastus, had given them to his pupil, Neleus, and they were concealed in a vault to safeguard them from theft, though they were damaged by dampness and worms. They were eventually recovered about 150 years later. For 150 years, there was absolutely no study of Aristotle. The study of these documents took place in centers that had been founded during Alexander's thirteen-year expedition to conquer the world. The writings of Aristotle were, therefore, scattered in different parts of the Middle East. Some of the writings had also come to Europe and influenced Augustine and the development of Christian doctrine. When Christianity arrived in the lands of the Middle East, Aristotle was again studied until Emperor Constantine ruled that Greek science should not be part of Christian culture. However, the study of Aristotle and Greek scientists was still preserved in places like Odessa and Gundishapur in Persia. Later, when the Arabs conquered that region, the teaching of Aristotle, which had been studied in these places and pondered over for centuries, was now available and became a rich source in the evolution of Islamic culture. The works of Aristotle were taken up with great fervor by Islamic scholars, but as Islam is a religion and not a philosophy, not all of Aristotle was appreciated. It was the philosophic and scientific content which inspired the scholars. Christianity and Islam thus came into a philosophical conflict which we will consider later.

Let us now imagine the life of a thirteenth century scholar. Traveling in a cart or on horseback between Rome and Paris, Aquinas might have covered twenty miles a day or as little as five miles in bad weather. He would be traveling on roads that were often in poor condition and dangerous, with no maps and no secure stopping places. Every journey was an adventure which he would not dare to do alone. Committing ideas to writing would be with a quill on parchment. Additional copies essential for the dissemination of ideas would be painstakingly copied by scribes. Books were kept in libraries and often chained to a table for security. However, the vast amount of knowledge possessed by individuals like Aquinas and Dante was stored in their memory, a capacity which must have been far more highly developed than we generally find today.

Apart from the basic living and working conditions, Aquinas faced a more important challenge in the rise and spread of Islamic scholarship. The conflict over the ownership of the holy places where Christ's life and death were enacted was disastrous for the Christian armies. By the eleventh century, Arabic science had made significant progress in astronomy, physics, chemistry, biology and mathematics. In general, Islamic culture was much superior to that of Christian Europe.

One of Islam's leading scholars was the Persian polymath, Avicenna, (980–1037). Living in Baghdad, that great cultural and commercial center of Arab civilization during its golden age, he covered every field of human knowledge. His studies, which were strongly influenced by the teachings of Aristotle, included physics, mathematics, astronomy, chemistry, and geology. He was a physician, a soldier as well as a statesman. After his death, that part of the Islamic world was taken over by the Islamic Turks and Baghdad began to decline as a leading cultural center. The Arabic impulse, however, now extended over North Africa, and eventually crossed into Spain. We have mentioned the attempt to conquer southern France by the armies of Islam, but that had been pushed back by the Franks. The Arabs settled in Spain and began to coexist with Christian and Jewish cultures to form a rich mix in cities like Cordoba and Toledo.

Another important Islamic scholar was Averroes (1126–1198) who was born in Cordoba. His extensive works in philosophy and theology also included commentaries on almost all of Aristotle's teachings which would present a major challenge for Aquinas.

In the tenth and eleventh centuries, many of the works of Aristotle which had previously been lost to Christian Europe, but existed in Arabic and Greek were now being translated into Latin. This rediscovery by Christian thinkers set the stage for a new cultural impulse in Christianity and European culture in general.

Aristotle had distinguished three levels of the soul, a vegetative soul (possessed by plants), a sensitive soul (possessed by animals in addition to the vegetative soul), and a rational soul (possessed only by human beings). In the rational soul, there were two elements, "Nous Poiêtikos" and "Nous Pathêtikos" (Nous = intellect or understanding.) The Nous Poiêtikos is the creative intelligence and Nous Pathêtikos is the passive intelligence. With the latter we know by looking at the world. The element in us which rises above such knowing, and is no longer dependent on sense perception, is Nous Poiêtikos. This intelligence is the highest level of Mind with which we can be creatively active. We have described this twofold nature of thinking, differently expressed, in the chapter on Aristotle.

The challenge faced by Aquinas concerned the nature of this creative intelligence. As understood by the scholastics and the Arab scholars, creative intelligence enables the human being to participate in the intelligence of the universe. The world is created in an intelligent way, by an intelligence pervading the universe. The human being has this capacity to perceive this world intelligence through his Nous Poiêtikos.

A question addressed by Avicenna: Was what happens to the soul after the human being dies? Is the soul immortal? It seemed to Avicenna that what we call the passive intelligence must die with it. But what about the Nous Poiêtikos? What about the active intelligence? Is that also extinguished with the death of the body? Avicenna concluded that the soul is immortal.

Some 150 years, later Averroes would disagree with Avicenna. He maintained that when the human being is in this intelligent communication with the universe, then it is the universe that is penetrating him from without. And when he dies, that disappears and with it also his immortal soul. In his view, when raindrops fall, they are all individual, but in the end, they all merge in the great ocean. All our individual intelligences are like that. This sets him in opposition to Avicenna. Once Averroes is translated from Arabic into Latin, the Catholic Church and Aquinas must confront this question: Is there no personal immortality? Does the soul live after death?

This is an important question in the development of consciousness. If the soul is mortal, it remains a servant of the Divine. God decides. Questions of individual development, personal responsibility, and relationship in freedom to Christ would no longer be valid. Aquinas felt bound to address the issue. He poses the question: "What decides that the human being is different from the animal creation?" The only thing that decides that is the human mind, the Nous Poiêtikos. "In the language of the Greeks, that is the human form (idea) and the form is the distinguishing shaping activity, which makes that what it is." Aquinas goes on to say that the creative form of the human, the identifying form of the human being, is the mind. And that mind is not involved in what we call the material world. It is quite impossible for all human beings to share one mind. "Mind," in knowing, uses no other tool than the mind itself. Therefore, the mind in its knowing is not using the body, only using the mind. The body is there to express it, but the mind itself, in its activity, is not using another tool like the body. The mind is, therefore, its own tool. It follows that a shared mind would do only one action. That is: all humans would be one "knower," engaged in one act of knowing for each known object. That is his response to Averroes.

We now have two theories of knowledge, that of Averroes and that of Aquinas. The crucial question concerns the immortality of the soul. For Averroes, there is a re-immersion of the human intellect in the universal intellect like drops of rainwater returning to the ocean where self-identity vanishes. Such a philosophy stands in opposition to the emergence of the personality, which we have considered in the case of Augustine. I had a personal experience of this question recently. I was returning home from London one evening and discovered that all trains to my destination were canceled and I was obliged to take a taxi. The journey took one hour. To pass the time, I opened a conversation with the driver who came from Pakistan and who was happy to share his views. As an opening gambit, I suggested that the influx of people from former British colonies was a pay-back for the country which once tried to own their country. He immediately picked up my suggestion as an opportunity to offer his understanding. He declared that everything is decided by God. Human beings do not decide. God decides. If the British colonized India, it was God who decided. If people from the East come to the West, it is God's decision. I was astonished at the firmness of his conviction and realized that we were potentially in the debate which engaged Aquinas.

A certain culmination is reached in the work of Aquinas. The stream of Aristotle has flowed together with Christian revelation. Reason and faith are the two faculties which enable humanity to be at home in the universe. The intellect feels itself still so united with nature that it can read it like a text. It is interesting to note that Aquinas considered the heart the bodily seat of the intellect, not the brain. Matthew Fox, in his book *Sheer Joy*, explores the work of Aquinas for a modern consciousness. I end this chapter with quotations from *Sheer Joy*. "Loving draws us more to things than knowledge does." In order to free oneself from judging the work of Aquinas from the viewpoint of the modern intellect, which deals in abstractions, I append the four paths on which Matthew Fox examines the work of Aquinas.

1. Via Positiva. The heart of exaltation, awe, wonder, and delight.
2. Via Negativa. The heart of silence, letting go, suffering, sorrow, grieving.
3. Via Creativa. The heart of passion, for creativity, birthing life and power in all its forms.
4. The heart that is compassion, moral outrage at injustice, making and healing, and the work that celebration entails and demands.

Aquinas fell silent some days before his death. It is reported that, on regaining consciousness, he said, "Such secrets have been revealed to me that all I have written appears as straw."

In centers of learning such as Chartres and the new universities founded during the time of the Scholastics in Padua, Paris, and Oxford, study was based on the Seven Liberal Arts. These consisted of the Trivium (Grammar, Dialectic, and Rhetoric) and the Quadrivium (Astronomy, Arithmetic, Geometry, and Music). In the fourteenth century, in line with the new change in approach, the Trivium had become "trivial" and abandoned, while the studies of the Quadrivium would be refashioned by the new thinking. The Nominalists' approach was sharpened by an English theologian, William of Ockham, who is famous for his "razor" which cuts out all proofs except the most direct and simplest. References to such concepts as spirit and faith have no value when direct evidence is available from the senses and clear thinking. This demolition of the Realist view made way for the modern scientific which was now emerging.

To understand changes, especially such monumental ones that began in Italy in the fourteenth century, the historian looks for causes. A change in the way one thinks is linked to developments in other fields. Through war and trade, new practices and new ideas migrate. By following the sequence, one may find the cause. The concept of an evolution in consciousness obliges one to reconsider the interconnectedness of events. The conquest of Byzantium by the Turks in 1453 and the flight of Greek scholars with manuscripts from the time of Plato onwards, are seen as important events to explain the Renaissance. However, the notion that a new way of thinking, a new way of perceiving, a new way of being in the world is emerging as if from an unknown source makes events like the conquest of Byzantium an accompaniment rather than a cause of the Renaissance.

The Renaissance is mostly associated with developments in painting, sculpture, and architecture. Perspective, classical themes as well as religious, new techniques, and an exact but external study of nature and the human body informed the new art. The medieval period has come to an end and with it the dominant position of Aristotle's teaching, which is discarded, and for a brief period, the writings of Plato inspire a fresh idealism.

Three inventions may be singled out as having a significant impact on this emerging age: The medieval fortress was vulnerable to the cannonballs projected by gunpowder brought into use in the fourteenth century. This enabled monarchs to dominate their powerful subjects and strengthened the unitary state. The nation now acquired a new loyalty and the use of Latin as a common language, which had given a certain unity to the culture of Western Europe, was now replaced by the vernacular languages we know today, Italian, French, English, etc.

The magnetic compass is also an important change-maker. It was widely used in Europe in the fifteenth century, though invented much earlier, and enabled ships to venture far from the coast. The printing press made books widely available and brought contemporary events, religious views, past and present literature in the vernacular language within the reach of those outside the Latin-speaking clerical circles.

Extraordinary artists like Leonardo, Michelangelo, and Raphael, explorers like Columbus and Vasco da Gama, inventors like Gutenberg and philosophers like Nicholas of Cusa illuminate the age. The term "Renaissance Man" can be applied to Leon Baptista Alberti, author, sociologist, artist, architect, poet, priest, linguist, and philosopher. He sums up the new confidence in these words: "When I investigate and when I discover that the forces of the heavens and the planets are within ourselves, then truly I seem to be living among the gods." And also, "A man can do all things if he but wills them."

The maxim of Protagoras, "Man is the measure of all things," is given new meaning and describes the pervading spirit. This is the prelude to the philosophical viewpoints of the seventeenth century. It is also the time of Luther and Calvin, who attack the hegemony of the Catholic Church. The consequence of this conflict is a war lasting thirty years (1618–1648), which devastated Germany for decades.

The seventeenth century was to reject the worldviews derived from the Greek and scholastic thinkers, and Francis Bacon represents the new approach. In common with Descartes and Spinoza, Bacon declares the need for a radical new beginning in philosophy. They also share the view that this demands a new basis in thinking, but in very different ways. Descartes' statement, "I think therefore I am," includes all the inner life, feelings, and wills, etc. For him the source of all knowledge is in the mind. As with Descartes, Spinoza's thought was shaped by the New Science. But his philosophy begins with what is ontological and logical, what is prior to everything else. His foundation is the divine and nature, and these two are one. Bacon, Descartes, and Spinoza, although their philosophies are very different, take their start from the nature of mind and are, as a result, called Rationalists.

Francis Bacon (1561 — 1626)

The writings of Francis Bacon will introduce us to radical ideas together with new social goals for philosophy and science which continue to resonate with our modern consciousness. Bacon's family belonged to the nobility, and he was brought up at the court of Queen Elizabeth I. As a student at Trinity College, Cambridge, he already knew the direction of his philosophy. For him, the studies of Plato and Aristotle were good to argue over but produced nothing for the benefit of humanity. In his first major work, the *Advancement of Learning*, he sets out his views on History, Poesy, and Philosophy (Memory, Imagination, and Reason). He added to the text over several years, so the final edition comprised two thick volumes. Bacon emphasized a practical not a contemplative approach to nature; the purpose of thinking is to benefit humanity and not merely to reflect on its nature. He became a lawyer and entered parliament at a very young age, then rose to power to become Lord Chancellor, the chief advisor of the king, James I. So, he had a supreme role in the government of England for several years until he was accused of corruption and receiving bribes and brought to court. He defended himself while accepting the charge: "Yes, I've received bribes. But I've never allowed them to interfere with my judgment." Although the court condemned him, he wasn't imprisoned, or even fined. But then he retired and dedicated himself to writing philosophy.

His ambitions were vast. He embarked on a book, which he never completed, called *Instauratio Magna* (Great Renewal). He aimed to reframe the whole question of how we have come to know the world and what it means. Aristotle maintained that a plant consists not only of the physical material substance, but also of the form (an inner shaping force in the plant). Bacon uses the Aristotelian concept but for him it means something different, it means a natural law such as we know in the laws of heat expansion. In philosophy, the use of words which have a specific content are frequently used with a different meaning by later scholars, which can lead to misunderstanding.

In order to discover these laws, the scientific experiment is the essential tool. This means to isolate the specific phenomenon to be studied and subject it to different experiments. "Different experiences" might be a justified expression, especially when applied to the living. Bacon writes of "torturing nature in order to gain power over it." Bacon's "knowledge is power" is now so familiar to us that we hardly question it. It seems natural. But, in fact, it has transformed nature into a mere source for the realization of our unfettered desires as well as sentimental entertainment.

Bacon contended, "Essentially all these past thinkers have been working out of thoughts from which you deduce one thing from a previous thought. My way of thinking is not like that." It's an inductive method, which means one looks at the facts, one looks at the particularities, and one gathers from that study the nature and function of the object. The deductive thinking, which allows for consideration of purpose and intentions (teleology), is no longer acceptable for the inductive reasoner.

Bacon also needed to exclude from his scientific method the Aristotelian concept of the final cause. An example from Aristotle is that of a bronze statue. What is its final cause? It is to celebrate a god. That is its final cause. The notion of the final cause was meaningful for Aristotelians when considering tree, animal, human being. Bacon said, "We get rid of final causes."

For Bacon, to ask after the purpose of a rat, or a lion, or a human being is not a valid question. The causes which now become very important are called efficient causes. What brings that about? Bacon is clearly determined to change the way of thinking. While he does not question the reality of the divine (he is not an atheist), he wants to leave aside all religious and metaphysical questions and focus his attention on understanding and acquiring power over the material world.

In the *Novum Organum* (replacing Aristotle's *Organum*), he sets out to contribute to this great renewal by providing a new means (organum = tool) for changing the world.

He describes four idols which are commonly worshiped and lead us into error. In order to search for the truth, one has to get rid of these four idols. The first one is the idol of the "tribe," all those ideas that we carry around with us in our language, in our customs, in our feelings, in all the sorts of things we like. We believe in things we like and we disbelieve things we don't like. One has to eliminate all of these from one's consciousness. You can't understand the world while you still carry around the idols of the "tribe." We also interpret the world, anthropomorphically ascribing to things in the world and to God a human expression, feelings, acts, thoughts. This anthropomorphic projection onto the universe is part of the idol of the "tribe."

The next one of which we must rid ourselves is the idol of the "cave." We are all living in our own little cave, and from there we see the world with our particular temperament, our particular experiences, our particular hopes and intentions, which, of course, shape the way we understand the world. Then there is the idol of the "marketplace." This idol is due to the influence of language which includes words for which there is no corresponding object. For example, words like "fortuna," (fortune) or "prima mobile" (the first mover, that which lies beyond the fixed stars and sets the whole starry configuration in movement) have no corresponding object. We must get rid of them. Words for which there is no corresponding sense-perceptible reality may exist in the marketplace but have no place in science.

The fourth is the idol of the "theatre." This comprises all those philosophical systems of the past that have been imposed on the world. To look at such systems, Plato's world or Aristotle's, is no different than looking at theatre. These stage performances only serve to obscure reality, and hence we must be rid of them. Only after one has got rid of these idols can one really face the serious question of how to grasp the world with understanding, and this understanding is acquired by practical experimentation. The contemplative approach of medieval scholars does not contribute to the realization of human benefits.

In one of his last and unfinished works, *New Atlantis,* Bacon describes his vision of a utopian society living on a mythical island and embodying all the traits of an enlightened people. Here generosity and enlightenment, dignity and splendor, piety and public spirit are common qualities, and the new science is practiced for the betterment of humankind.

Although Bacon described the function of the experiment, he rarely engaged in experiments himself, but rather set out a method which others should follow. During a journey in snow and ice, Bacon decided to find out if a chicken is preserved by being stuffed with ice. As a result, he caught a cold and died at the age of sixty-five.

Bacon was known as a humanist whose writings reveal a vast range of knowledge. This encouraged the notion that he may even have been the author of the plays attributed to Shakespeare. The supporters of this view maintain that the actor from Stratford lacked the knowledge, experience and background to be their author. I think there is no firm basis for such a belief. His passionate interest in and deep understanding of the human condition explain why he is regarded as one of the outstanding figures of his time. His scientific attitude is summed up in the following lines from *The Advancement of Learning*:

> All knowledge and wonder (which is the seed of knowledge) is an impression of pleasure in itself. If a man will begin with certainties, he shall end in doubts, but if he will be content to begin with doubts he shall end in certainties.

René Descartes (1596 — 1650)

René Descartes also shares the conviction with Bacon that a new beginning in philosophy is needed. However, his response is very different. Descartes is a man of his time. A man of fragile health, Descartes was introduced to mathematics and physics, including the work of Galileo (1564–1642), during his studies in the Jesuit military college at La Flèche in the Loire region. He concluded his studies in law to satisfy his father's wishes. However, in 1618, dissatisfied with his life in France, he moved to Holland and joined the Protestant forces as a mercenary in the Dutch army. During this time he undertook training in military engineering, thus furthering his studies in physics and mathematics. The following year, Descartes entered the military service of the Catholic Duke of Bavaria. Descartes then returned to France, but in his early thirties, he again left for Holland where he could work on his new philosophy beyond the reach of the Inquisition.

His ultimate search is for a meaningful basis for understanding the world without including previous ideas and assumptions. He publishes a number of treatises on optics and refraction and also on meteors. Finally, he decides to give himself space and time to think out the basic questions.

Descartes describes in the first of his six *Meditations* the place and time that his revelation came to him. He is in Holland, lodged in an inn, where he sits in his dressing gown with no company to distract him. The weather is rather cold and his room is heated by an enclosed stove.

He addresses the question, "What can I really know that is free of any possible error?" He cannot begin with the sense objects around him as their existence can be doubted. He decides he must look within for a secure footing, and so he proceeds to examine all propositions that are believed to be true, but if they can be subject to any doubt, they must be discarded. Following this skeptical method, he questions how he might know that his experience is not just some elaborate dream and that he is not being deceived by a malevolent devil. As he is being deceived about everything, how can he actually state, "No, that isn't true?" He even goes so far to ask, "Well, couldn't God deceive us?" But there's one thing he can be sure about. There is a "thinking" going on. "I am thinking." That's the only thing he can be sure about. He can doubt the existence of his own body, but he cannot doubt that he is thinking. From this position he sets out to construct a worldview free from error. He is thus known as the founder of Rationalism.

Descartes' philosophy is presented in two publications, *Meditations on First Philosophy* and *Discourse on Method.* In the fourth *Discourse,* he takes the reader through the questions and doubts that he needs to deal with:

> I resolved to pretend that nothing which had ever entered my mind was any more true than the illusions of my dreams. I then became aware that, while I decided thus to think that everything is false, it follows necessarily that I who thought thus must be something; and observing that truth: I think, therefore I am (cogito ergo sum) was so certain and so evident that sceptics could not shake it, I judged I could accept it as the first principle of the philosophy I was seeking.

The philosophy was immediately attacked by his contemporaries as promoting atheism and laying the foundation for materialism. He was seen as fostering a cold, calculating, and rationalistic view of the human being and that the extended world is soulless and purely mechanical, thus providing a basis for modern materialism. His use of skeptical arguments for doubting has been challenged. For example, he also expresses his primary thought as I doubt therefore I am (dubito ergo sum). However, in spite of flaws, different elements of his philosophy have continued to influence modern thinkers. Having proved the existence of the thinking ego, Descartes has to investigate the sense world to establish its reality. In the second *Meditation,* he considers a piece of wax. Its taste, color, perfume, shape and size are evident. It is hard and cold. If one heats it, then all these impressions disappear. The same wax remains. So, how does he recognize the one in the other with such clarity? "The action by which one perceives the wax is not an act of sight, or touch etc., and has never been, although it seemed so hitherto, but only an intuition of the mind." He concludes, "We perceive bodies only by the understanding which is in us and not by the senses." The real source of knowledge lies in the mind.

He then states that the idea of perfection is a product of mind and therefore must exist. As a consequence, the existence of God as a perfect being is proved.

Descartes has proved the existence of mind and of God, but he is unable to trust all that comes from the senses. As a perfect God may not deceive, the object world must also exist but outside the proven worlds. This gives them a purely mechanical existence. The human body, the animal and plants have therefore a machine-like nature. This notion will resonate today in biology.

These thoughts lead to the concept that the world consists of two kinds of "stuff," mind stuff and body or sensory stuff. How they interact was not resolved by Descartes. Mind has become man's supreme faculty but has lost its roots. The isolated body is reduced to a mechanical functioning, a thing to manipulate.

Galileo had identified mathematics as the supreme tool to investigate the external world and provide true knowledge. He declared, "Mathematics is the language in which God has written the universe." Science had to be based on what can be measured, such as extension, weight, number, and movement, the so-called primary qualities. The perceptions of color, smell, taste, and touch, being unquantifiable, are then called secondary qualities that only reside in the observer. Hence mathematics assumed a prime role in scientific research. Descartes was therefore contributing to the development of mathematics. Contemporary thinkers might criticize his philosophy, but his contribution to science could not be doubted.

Pascal, his contemporary, also a mathematician and scientist, was a strong opponent of Descartes' philosophy.

Pascal is mostly known for his *Pensées,* an extraordinary collection of thoughts arranged on themes which have been an inspiration to many readers with their insight into the human condition. As a scientist, he studied air pressure at different altitudes and made the first barometer. In mathematics, he laid the foundation of projective geometry and the laws of probability. The seventeenth century was to prove an exceedingly productive period for science and mathematics, culminating in the crowning achievements of Isaac Newton.

The energetic ruler of Sweden, Queen Christina, invited Descartes to her palace in Stockholm in order to study philosophy and other subjects under him. Descartes spent a year in Sweden in spite of the climate and the requirements of the Queen. The cold winter did not suit him nor did study at 5 a.m., which the Queen, an early riser, insisted on. Descartes was accustomed to rise at midday and begin his work in the evening and continue through the night. The result was that Descartes fell ill and died in Sweden.

Baruch Spinoza (1632 — 1677)

S pinoza was born in Amsterdam into a Portuguese-Jewish family. His grandparents had left Portugal to escape the Inquisition and sought a new life in Holland and the relatively liberal Dutch society where they could once again practice their Jewish customs. His father, a successful merchant, recognized his son's intellectual gifts at an early age and placed him in the hands of the finest teachers, expecting that he would become a worthy rabbi. When Spinoza was twenty-two, his father died. There followed a family dispute about inheritance which Spinoza won. With the exception of a four-poster bed and surrounding curtain, he gave away his entitlement in favor of his sister. This was characteristic of Spinoza, who cared nothing for the comforts of this world and lived out his life in frugal simplicity. As a skilled lens-grinder, he was able to sustain himself and devote his energies to his true task.

He had already recognized that he had to develop his thinking to understand the world and the human being's place in it. First of all, he examined and rejected the conventional notions current in society. This brought him into conflict with his family and the whole Jewish community. His conception of God offended Calvinists, who were the majority Christians in Holland, as well as the Jews. In one of his first publications, the treatise *On the Improvement of the Understanding*, he examines the goals which life offered him if he so chooses, and shows what he would lose if he embarked on the life he was drawn to. Riches, fame, and pleasure are the three temptations which he finally rejects because of unsatisfactory elements concealed in them.

The writings of Descartes gave Spinoza the necessary ground in thinking for the pursuit of his own philosophy. Mathematics and mathematical thinking, in which one intuits a truth and then deduces further truths from it, is an essential requirement. To recognize the truths of geometry, one does not look outside for proof. That the angles of a triangle equal two right angles is established by the mind, independent of any reference to sense impressions. It is this kind of thinking which Spinoza will use to grapple with the problem he has set himself.

Descartes had distinguished two "stuffs," thought and extension. Thought belongs to the inner world, separate from it is the extended mechanical world. Spinoza asks the question, "Where must one begin in order to build a true picture of the world?" He concludes that there are many thoughts which tempt us to select this one or that but a satisfactory cornerstone must be something which can stand by itself and needs nothing else for its being. He calls this something "substance." There can only be one such substance and this is God. He proceeds like Euclid, who starting from given premises derives further truths by necessity. Having begun with the one substance which the thinker has to acknowledge, there cannot be anything existing outside itself. If there cannot be another substance, then everything else must be in the substance, must be one of its attributes, in Spinoza's language. There are two such attributes, one when one looks out at the world, the other when one looks inward. The first is extension, the second, thinking. The human contains both attributes in their being: in his body, extension; in his soul, thinking. When they think, it is the divine substance which thinks, when they act, it is this substance, the body attribute that acts. The ego is anchored in the divine substance. In this picture, there is no place for absolute freedom for the human being, for they are no more to be credited with the initiative of their actions and thought than a stone in flight with its movement. The agent of everything is the one substance. The human being has only a relative freedom when they see themselves not as an individual but know themselves as one with the one substance.

So, for Spinoza, the ground of all world events was in God. All that happens comes from that source according to necessary laws, in the same way that mathematical truths are deduced from axioms. He considered human desires and deeds to be elements in the world just as lines and planes are elements in geometry. At the same time, a thought is more than a perception; it is an experience. He does not acknowledge good and evil as such; nor does he acknowledge the whole realm of morals and aesthetics.

Spinoza's world is that of a contemplative. God and Nature are the same. Love of God is not a religious sentiment or directed to a personal deity. It is more like the pleasure and mental satisfaction which accompanies a scientist's explanation of the universe.

It is now easy to understand the condemnation of Spinoza's work which came from representatives of both the Christian and Jewish faiths. Their God was made in the image of man, with thoughts, feelings, and actions. Their God demanded obedience and favored those who kept His laws. At twenty-three, Spinoza was excommunicated from the Jewish community on the charge of atheism, and it was as an atheist as well as a unique thinker that he gained notoriety across Europe.

In his major publication, *The Ethics* (published after his death), Spinoza begins with the nature of substance and from that he demonstrates the truth about God, nature, and the human being and the highest principles of society, religion and the good life. The book is written in the form of a geometric proof starting with Definitions, Axioms, and then Propositions, which are interspersed with notes to the reader. While his exposition may not be easy to follow because of his unique method and the concepts he employs, Spinoza may also be seen as thoroughly modern in his outlook, his ideas appearing in the modern concept of Gaia as well as much New Age thinking. Arnold Zweig has written in his study of Spinoza:

> When we read that the free will of man is to be traced back to the ignorance which determines it and that real freedom arises rather in the measure man frees himself from his passions to unite himself with God in contemplation, we see the faint smile and melancholy eyes of that lonely man who went out to the world to radiate light.

Spinoza was known to be both humble and considerate in his relations with his fellow citizens. His unique contribution was to assert the triumph of reason and abide by its dictates. In a letter to a student, while acknowledging that he had not written the best philosophy, he stated, "I do know that I think the true one."

The three seventeenth century philosophers, Bacon, Descartes, and Spinoza, shared the view that past thinking no longer served the needs of their time. The age could accept only what comes from the individual's thinking. For Plato, answers were obtained from a heightened awareness and the Socratic dialogue. During the middle ages when Christianity became the dominant influence in Western Europe, philosophy became a servant to the religious impulse. Nature was seen as a text that could be read by a mind educated to the task. In the fifteenth century, philosophy began to free itself from religious beliefs.

The new thinkers place their individual understanding center stage, challenging traditional forms. They are not just interpreters but shapers of the world. To the observance of nature is added the active investigation of its hidden forces and thus new technical possibilities. The paradox is that as the human being is no longer seen as the center and purpose of the universe, their thought and will becomes more powerfully engaged in creating change, in forging their own future.

The seventeenth century is also marked by other significant events and scientific achievements. In Britain, the Civil War and the execution of Charles I seemed a final judgment on the rule of hereditary kingship. It was followed by a decade of Puritan dictatorship under Oliver Cromwell. On his death, the hereditary monarchy was restored. The democratic ideas which the Digger movement and others had hoped to realize after the death of Charles I were ignored and the concentration of government was oriented to the creation of wealth in which colonies were to play a vital role. In 1665 the Great Plague devastated the city of London, and the following year the Great Fire destroyed a large part of the city. Many of the buildings were of wood so a new city rose on the ashes of the old. The architect Christopher Wren was responsible for a new St Paul's Cathedral and a large number of churches, each of a unique design. Were these events a prelude to a new political and social journey for Britain? A dark shadow accompanied any hopeful thinking. The Royal African Company was formed to buy and transport slaves from Africa to the English colonies and dependencies in the Caribbean to work on sugar plantations. The king and his ministers actively supported this policy which remained in force throughout the eighteenth century.

The scientific discoveries of the seventeenth century affected the general view of the world. Torricelli, a follower of Galileo, created a vacuum – a simple mercury barometer – which questioned Aristotle and the medieval maxim that "Nature abhors a vacuum." The word "gas" was invented by a Dutch scientist as a result of the discovery that air has several forms and these have weight. The expansion of solids, liquids, and gases by heat was also explored. On the night when Cromwell died, there was a great wind blowing across East Anglia and a fourteen-year-old boy was intent on measuring its force. First, he ran into the wind and jumped. Having measured the length of his jump he ran and jumped with the wind at his back and measured again. This enabled him to calculate the relative force of the wind. The boy was Isaac Newton.

Newton (1642–1726) is considered one of the foremost scientific intellects of all time. Before he was thirty, he had laid the basis for his work in physics and mathematics. His experiments of a ray of light passing through a prism were accepted as evidence that white light was a mixture of the colored rays. The cause of the fall of an apple and the force which maintains the moon in its orbit are the same force of gravity. He studied the colors that appear in thin films like in oil and soap bubbles and managed to measure their thickness. He maintained that light consisted of minute particles. His research laid the basis for a worldview that the universe is determined by mechanical forces. In mathematics, he developed the solutions to the problems of curvature with the invention of calculus. Leibnitz had also made a similar solution and a jealous rivalry was stirred up between the two. *The Principia* is the title which Newton gave to the book he eventually published containing a description of his achievements. It emerged later that he was a student of alchemy and also wrote on Judeo-Christian prophecy in which the measurements of the Solomon temple given in the bible formed a basis.

The three philosophers selected to represent the thinking of the eighteenth century are British, and although they arrive at very different conclusions, they share a common focus based in sense experience. Locke maintained that all knowledge is acquired initially from the senses. All forms of nature can be explained mechanically by matter in motion and the impact of one body on another. Berkeley accepted the world that enters our consciousness but denied the existence of inanimate matter and sought to demonstrate that nothing exists except spiritual activity in God's infinite mind and in human minds. Hume is the supreme skeptic. All our ideas are copied from our impressions. It is not reason which connects our ideas, but habits of mind. However hard we try, we can never get away from ourselves and our perceptions.

John Locke (1632 — 1704)

Locke was born into a Puritan family and was a student in London and may have been present at the execution of Charles I. He wrote his major work at the end of his life, so the influence of his book in four volumes *An Essay Concerning Human Understanding* belongs to the eighteenth century. He made an intensive study of medicine and then considered becoming a diplomat. He joined the household of Lord Shaftesbury as physician and secretary and later was elected to the Royal Society founded in 1660. There he would meet leading scientists, Newton, Boyle, and Hooke, known at the time as Natural Philosophers. Christopher Wren would also be there. At some stage he got involved in an argument, which the different parties were unable to resolve. Locke gave himself the task of finding out on what objects our understandings were or were not fitted to deal with.

The following propositions by Locke were later to be adopted by scholars in Britain and America and promoted by Voltaire and other revolutionaries on the Continent.

1. The established opinion that we have innate principles I shall prove to be false. Can ideas of color be innate in a creature with sight or impressions of nature with the faculty to attain knowledge of them?

2. There is an assumption that certain principles universally agreed upon are brought into the world at birth. If there are such ideas it is no proof that they are there by universal consent if it can be shown that the agreement has been reached in another way.

3. In fact, there are no such principles to which mankind gives its universal consent.

4. Men assent to these principles when they come to the use of reason.

5. The capacity to know is innate, all knowledge is acquired and initially through the sense experience.

For Locke the mind is like a blank sheet of paper (tabula rasa) which is written on by impressions of the senses both outer and inner. Our faculty of reflection enables us to combine those simple ideas constructed by the senses into complex ideas.

What does Locke mean by idea? In his *Essay*, Book 2, Chapter 2, "Simple Ideas," he states:

> Though the qualities that affect our senses are in the things themselves so united and blended that there is no separation, no distance between them; yet it is plain, the ideas they produce in the mind enter by the senses simple and unmixed. These simple ideas, the materials of all our knowledge, are suggested and furnished to the mind only by those two ways above mentioned.

Then Locke maintains that these bodies produce ideas in us manifestly by impulse, the only way we can conceive to operate in. Complex ideas arise when several simple ideas are combined by the mind. It is clear that Locke uses the concept of 'idea' in a new way, wholly different from the rationalist tradition.

For Locke, Nature is a mechanical system in which all phenomena can be explained by matter in motion and the impact of one body on another. Matter is passive and composed of particles which move in an empty space. These particles are called primary and have properties: they are extended, solid, of a particular shape, and moving or at rest. They combine to form objects of the sense world. Other properties like colors, taste, and smell, which are deemed to be secondary, he calls ideas. He writes, "As they are sensations or perceptions in our understanding, I call them ideas." Secondary qualities do not really belong to the objects outside us; they are subjective effects produced in our minds by the primary qualities in bodies. Our knowledge of material substance depends heavily on the secondary qualities, by reference to which we name them, while their real inner natures derive from their non-sensory part.

This view that science gives us is real knowledge compared to that corresponding to our human reaction to the world. The human being is in Locke's philosophy an object among objects and should be studied as such. Towards the end of the *Essay*, confidence in the certainty of knowledge appears in the difficulty which exists in seeing the connection between primary and secondary qualities. Later he admits that it is vain to search for the 'forms' of material substances or to verify the corpuscular theory. He wrote that certainty and demonstration in these things we must not pretend to.

In other writings, Locke supports liberal values in his condemnation of the hereditary principle and of slavery. As he was for a time a major investor in the Royal African Company, which funded the slave trade, he is accused of hypocrisy. With Lord Shaftesbury, he was engaged in the setting up of a constitution for Carolina, a new colony in America. The constitution created a feudal aristocracy and gave masters absolute rights over slaves. As Locke later opposed all forms of political oppression, it is not easy to make any final judgment. His views on education are expressed in a letter he wrote in which he states the belief that education makes the human being, and more fundamentally, that the mind is "an empty cabinet" or a tabula rasa. He argued that the associations of ideas that one makes when young are the foundation of the self; they are what first mark the tabula rasa.

Finally, his philosophy did not get in the way of his faith in God and Christianity and absolute confidence in the Bible in all its contents. Locke was a loyal member of the Anglican Church, which must have been reassuring to many who accepted his philosophy in spite of the contradictions.

George Berkeley (1685 — 1753)

Berkeley was a priest of the protestant Church of Ireland. He was increasingly concerned about religious questions and wrote a defence of Christianity. His missionary zeal induced him to attempt to found a missionary training center in Bermuda encouraged by the promise of the necessary funds. He moved to Rhode Island and lived there for several years waiting for the government to send the funds. When it became clear this would not happen, he returned to London where he published his *Defence Of Christianity*. He married and had seven children. He was appointed Bishop of Cloyne in Ireland and lived there until his retirement in 1752. He was highly esteemed for the care he gave to the Protestant and Catholic families in his diocese.

Berkeley's philosophy is described in *A Treatise Concerning the Principles of Human Knowledge* (1710). Like Locke he is considered an empiricist, that is, one who asserts that all knowledge is based on experience derived from the senses. Nevertheless, he is Locke's strongest critic and arrives at a very different worldview. Both try to give a coherent account of the "outer" and "Inner" worlds in such a way that the truth can be verified in ordinary everyday experience without using metaphysical ideas or occult entities beyond the boundaries of the senses. In the introduction to the *Treatise,* he writes:

> Philosophy being nothing else but the study of wisdom and truth, it may with reason be expected that those who have spent most time and pains in it should enjoy a greater calm and serenity of mind, a greater clearness and evidence of knowledge and be less disturbed with doubts and difficulties than other men.

Berkeley, however, observes that the "Illiterate bulk of humanity" are mostly at ease and undisturbed and face the world with common sense. "As soon as we depart from sense and instinct to follow the light of a superior principle, to reason and reflect on the nature of things, a thousand scruples spring up in our minds concerning which before we seemed fully to comprehend."

The chief culprits are our use of abstract ideas and our failure to understand the nature of language. He dismisses Locke's notion about the difficulty of forming abstract ideas. Berkeley accepts abstractions as convenient means of grouping things that are alike but not abstractions which contain things that are incompatible. For example, he questions the concept "animal" as distinct from "human" on the basis that our only evidence for difference is that humans have abstract ideas, which animals lack. This is founded on the observation that the distinction is grounded not on the animal's lack of language but on the false assumption that animals have no abstract ideas, which cannot be proved. In other words, we use abstract ideas when they are no longer simply expressions of groups of like things. For Berkeley, the wealth of ideas evolved by Aquinas and the "Schoolmen" are all in vain. Language has many other uses than the communication of abstract ideas. It can convey at the same time all kinds of feelings, not necessarily intended by the speaker or writer. Reference to an abstract situation may arouse fear although no actual cause for fear is described. Language is the source of much of our failure to apprehend the nature of the world we live in. Of course, language has given us the vast stock of knowledge we possess. "But at the same time, it must be owned that most parts of knowledge have been strangely perplexed and darkened by the abuse of words."

Berkeley begins the *Treatise* by pointing out that in addition to all objects and qualities that exist, there likewise is something which knows or perceives them, and then applies will, imagination, or memory to them.

> This something, this perceiving active entity, I call mind, spirit, soul, or myself. I don't mean by these any one of my ideas but something quite distinct from them, wherein they exist, or, which is the same thing whereby they are perceived; for the existence of an idea or object consists in being perceived.

This is the essence of Berkeley's theory. To clarify the statement further, Berkeley goes on to write:

> Everyone will allow that neither thoughts, nor passions nor ideas formed by the imagination exist without the mind. It seems equally obvious that the various sensations or ideas imprinted on the senses, however blended or combined together, cannot exist other than in a mind perceiving them. "Esse est percipi." To exist is to be perceived.

This central theme is elaborated in the *Treatise* and may be summed up in the following way: The impressions that the things and events appear to produce on the human soul take place in reality within the soul itself. When I see red, I must bring redness into my being within myself. When I feel warm, the warmth lives within me. So it is with all things that I apparently receive from outside. Except for those elements I produce within myself, I know nothing whatsoever about the external things. So, it makes no sense to speak about things that consist of material substance, for I know only what appears in my mind as something spiritual. What I call a rose is something mental or spiritual, that is a perception experienced in my mind. So, we only perceive what is spiritual, and when I notice that I am affected by something from outside, then it can only be caused by spiritual or mental influences. Material bodies cannot cause such effects, and there are only spirits in the world that influence each other.

Berkeley's theory presupposes that what is not perceived does not exist, which seems absurd. His solution is that all is in the mind of God, which must make God the perceiver as well as the creator of the world. In Locke and Berkeley, the materialist and the spiritual views confront each other.

Our third empiricist, David Hume, proceeds to undermine all faith in any certain knowledge by the application of his skeptical method.

David Hume (1711 — 1776)

Hume was born in Edinburgh, where he studied law and soon realized his preference was philosophy and that he had sufficient means to pursue it. He writes of a moment of illumination which confirmed his vocation. He went to France and there wrote his masterpiece, *A Treatise on Human Nature*. He published it on his return to London, but there was little response to it. In his words, "It fell dead-born from the press." He continued to publish essays but the work that drew attention to him was *The History of England*. He was now recognized as a leading writer appreciated in France and Germany as well as in Britain. He continued to expand his philosophical ideas, and these were eventually published as *An Inquiry Concerning Human Understanding*.

He proposed to build a complete system of the sciences on an entirely new foundation, in his view, the only one that can stand with any security. This new foundation he expressed in the statement, "The experience of the senses is the basis and corrective of our knowledge." I have used citations from the *Treatise on Human Nature*, Hume's first attempt to publish his philosophy, in addition to the *Inquiry*. His approach, as we shall see, is that of the skeptic. "What any common man means by a hat or a shoe is no more than a collection and succession in time of sensible qualities." No need for a substratum of matter or mind to hold the ideas together as required by Locke and Berkeley. Impressions, not Locke's simple ideas, are what we meet at first when we relate to the world according to Hume. "It is our job to get the idea as clear as possible before attempting philosophy." In other words, ideas are copied from our impressions and we are able to connect them. This is a crucial aspect in Hume's empiricist approach.

> There is a secret tie or union among particular ideas, which causes the mind to join them more frequently together. This is not caused by any rational or theoretical principle, but it is too

obvious to escape observation that different ideas are connected together.

The Association of Ideas is an essential principle in Hume's system. There are three principles of connection, resemblance, contiguity, and cause and effect. Cause and effect are by far the strongest. Causation is also the associative principle which takes us beyond the evidence of memory and our senses.

His notion of impressions which bring ideas into the mind and the associations of ideas are the essential basis for an intelligible and successful investigation of human nature. What else claims to be necessary is a product of the "Imagination." Belief or assent is always present with the memory and the senses, and it is their "vivacity" which distinguishes them from imagination. Hume's "Imagination" has a very different meaning from the Romantic imagination which, at that time, was taking hold of poets and dramatists.

Hume's style is to confront the reader with challenging and often brief statements. He seems to assume that these are evident and need no proof. Everything that he asserts can be traced back to perceptions and any attempt to find a cause for these he rejects. He makes many acute observations on the ideas of other empiricists. A special one is that cause and effect is not a phenomenon like others which make impressions on the mind. We don't observe causality; we add it to our sense experience. The importance of this observation will be addressed later by Immanuel Kant. Hume explains that we add causality to our sense experience not because of reason but because of habit, experience, and belief. Expecting that fire will warm is not just conceiving of its warming but believing that it will warm. Belief is a lively conception produced by habit.

He also maintains that the notion of causation is produced where an object is followed by a similar second object and also an object followed by another whose appearance conveys the thought of the first. Only experience can teach us the nature and bounds of cause and effect, and enable us to infer the existence of one object from the existence of another. Since we all have limited experience, our conclusions should be always tentative, modest, reserved, and cautious.

Hume is famous for his attack on the self, on the notion that the self has substance. Hume does not accept that there are substances. We receive "impressions" but do not speculate on their cause. For Hume, impressions exist in themselves and have no need of "substance." What we call the soul is a collection of data, a stream of feelings, thoughts, images, and percepts loosely connected. The mind is nothing but "a bundle or collection of different perceptions." He refutes our tendency to ascribe identity to what is in fact a set of wholly discrete impressions since we have a natural propensity to imagine there is unity and identity which do not exist. He always had a contempt for Christianity and all existing religions. However, he did not think of himself as an atheist. His complaint against religions was that they did not offer an explanation of the world as we know it and gave no ground for belief in an afterlife. But he also did not accept the arrogant views of the French, "les philosophes," who claimed their atheism was a superior knowledge of an unknown world, but in fact they were just as ignorant as everyone else.

Hume considered the question of morality as belonging to "the science of man." The Newtonian methods of philosophizing are as applicable to the moral as to the physical sciences. "Occult hypotheses should be dispensed with; experience must be the arbiter." I observe that the limitations of Hume's understanding of the human being reach deep into modern culture, especially in education.

His writings became popular for their direct assault on religion and the aristocratic establishment. His rejection of all metaphysics and knowledge not derived from the physical senses was in tune with an increasingly secular society.

In the year of his death, he wrote *My Own Life*, a brief account of the important events and his reflections on them. This excerpt from it may be of interest in revealing the character of one described by Isaiah Berlin as the greatest and most revolutionary of British philosophers.

> I was a man of mild dispositions, of command of temper, of an open social, and cheerful humor and of great moderation in all my passions. My friends never had occasion to vindicate any one circumstance of my character and conduct. I cannot say there is no vanity in making this funeral oration of myself, but I hope it is not a misplaced one; and that this is a matter of fact which is easily cleared and ascertained.

His views contain a basic contradiction, like those of Locke and Berkeley. He reduces all ideas to impressions or mere habits of mind yet appeals to the thinking faculty in the reader as understood before he proceeds to diminish it. He substitutes for the concept of self a medley of impressions, yet in his last thoughts on his own life, he reveals the characteristics of a fully conscious self.

I have outlined the thoughts of three British philosophers and left out of consideration the work of thinkers in France, Germany, and elsewhere. Montesquieu, Rousseau, and Voltaire were important thinkers who prepared the ground for the tempestuous events in the French Revolution and hence in Europe at the end of the eighteenth century. Philosophy in Germany was also vigorous, and I shall next describe the work of Immanuel Kant whose thoughts strongly influenced the nineteenth century. One of his declared intentions was to rid philosophy of the defects inherent in Rationalism and Empiricism.

Immanuel Kant (1724 — 1804)

K ant was the son of a cobbler who lived all his life in Königsberg (a Baltic Sea town – formerly in East Prussia – now present-day Kaliningrad, Russia). Kant never traveled further than fifty miles from his home, and it is said that one could set one's watch by his daily walk across Königsplatz.

His writings present a challenge for any reader due to the complexity of his conceptual world, his use of specialized vocabulary, and the intricate interweaving of his thoughts. In spite of this, he became the outstanding philosopher of the nineteenth century.

He studied the rationalists, Descartes and Spinoza, and the empiricists, Locke, Berkeley, and Hume, and observed certain flaws in the two systems and set about eliminating these and providing a new and more thorough ground for understanding the world. To appreciate his achievements, let us briefly review how 'ideas" were conceived in previous ages. For Plato, the idea is 'above" the phenomenon, for Aquinas the idea is 'in" the phenomenon, and in the age beginning in sixteenth and seventeenth centuries, the idea is 'separate" from the phenomenon and thinking is a personal product.

In the large perspective, consciousness manifests an evolutionary change. From the human being participating in nature there emerges the human being as a separated observer of nature. The question, 'How do I know the world?" implies in the questioner a certain disposition or attitude, which includes dismissing certain assumptions and adopting others. These assumptions will affect the way the questioner proceeds to think on the question. Thinking will depend on the ground the thinker assumes.

Here am I. Nature and the world are over there. Is my primary experience one of a 'subjective mind," of the I, or of an 'objective world" which surrounds me? The two, mind and world, don't just flow together. Everywhere I turn, I am confronted with questions. If my 'subjective mind" and the 'world out there" flowed together, there would be no gap between understanding and perceiving an object. From its beginning, philosophy has undertaken to find a bridge over this gap.

To bridge the gap, Descartes started with the mind, the ego. Cogito ergo sum. The gap had already appeared with the nominalists, who considered the name as a label for a thing and not a concept integral to the object.

For the empiricists, a stove and its warmth were never in doubt. Did the world make sense by itself or did the observer have to contribute to the meaning? The mind's capacity to count, weigh, and measure was all that was needed. Newton's research on gravity, light, and the laws of moving bodies supported this position. When the new science discarded the former symbolic imagery of the universe, nature became disenchanted. That is a way of saying that the sensory qualities that once thrilled through nature are unreal and products of the human brain. Moral and religious beliefs would also have to be tested for evidence like any sensory object.

Locke's claim that there is nothing in the mind that is not first in the senses set the boundary for knowledge. Hume, however, noticed that cause and effect are not observed by the senses. The observer decides on the basis of habit, memory, or the closeness of the two events.

Kant was struck by Hume's statement on causation, which woke him, as he wrote, from his "dogmatic slumber" and at the age of fifty-seven set him on a new philosophic inquiry.

Kant was more in sympathy with the rationalists, who developed metaphysical systems as opposed to the empiricists who based their philosophy on experience. If causality is not a sense experience, then it must be a product of the mind. The implication is that the appearance of the external world depends on the way the mind is constructed. Kant realized that rationalists and empiricists are one-sided, and he needed to find a way to go beyond both. This would need a Copernican revolution in philosophy. Copernicus (1473–1543) revolutionized astronomy by placing the sun at the center of our universe and demonstrating that the appearance of the celestial world depended on the position and movement of the observer on earth. Similarly, might the world of appearances also depend on the construction of the human mind? This question becomes, for Kant, not how do we come to understand the world, but how the world comes to be understood by us.

Hume's skeptical philosophy was a challenge to Kant. It had a certain validity, but the conclusions were contrary to his beliefs on the range of human understanding, on the soul and God, and on morality. To understand Kant's resolution, it is necessary to explain terms he uses to distinguish different types of truth or knowledge. The terms are in Latin, the language in which philosophical and scientific works were written.

Our knowledge depends on what our senses reveal to us. These are "a posteriori," that is, knowledge comes after the sense experience.

We also get knowledge from our power to reason with no prior sense experience. (Three angles in a triangle make 180 degrees). These are "a priori."

Knowledge may also be Analytic or Synthetic.

Analytic: for example: The ear is the organ of hearing. The subject (ear) is explained by the predicate (the organ of hearing).

Synthetic: for example: The sense of hearing exists in fish. In this sentence the predicate is totally different from the subject.

Using these criteria, Kant identified three types of legitimate statements of fact:

1. Analytic a priori: definitions, logical truths, e.g. parallel lines meet at the horizon. Philosophy is the love of wisdom.

2. Synthetic a priori: knowledge with no basis in sense perception. Examples are: three angles of a triangle = 180°. The soul is immortal. Love is everlasting.

3. Synthetic a posteriori: facts we get to know through our senses which are reasonably certain, e.g., oak trees lose their leaves in winter.

Kant considered analytic a posteriori statements to be self-contradictory. He understood that synthetic a posteriori statements would need to overcome the skeptical argument, namely, that what appears is no evidence of what is real. So, to gain a secure foundation for knowledge, he focused on synthetic a priori statements, those whose truth could be ascertained independently of sense impressions.

His major work *The Critique of Pure Reason,* published in 1781, is a critique of the rationalists who try to justify metaphysics on the basis of reason. It also examines the issue of causality prompted by Hume's observation. In his *Prolegomena,* Kant makes the following comment on Hume's view of causality:

> How is it possible, says that acute man, that when a concept is given me, I can go beyond it and connect with it another, which is not contained in it, in such a manner as if the latter necessarily belonged to the former?

The issue is, for example, the sun causing a stone to get warm. Hume understood it as follows:

> Only experience can give us such a connection and all that vaunted necessity, or, what is the same thing, all cognition assumed to be a priori is nothing but a long habit of accepting something as true, and hence of mistaking subjective necessity for objective.

Kant goes on to show that the concept of cause is a pure concept of the understanding totally separate from all possible perception. While Hume argues that experience is the source of all our ideas, Kant counters that it must be the structure of the mind which makes experience possible. If I say, "The sun warms the stone," I add to the perception a concept of the understanding, namely, a cause which connects the concept of sunshine to that of heat as a necessary consequence. The synthetic statement becomes universally valid, that is, objective. Kant sums it up in this way: "The understanding does not derive its laws (a priori) from nature, but prescribes them to nature."

Kant's next step is to show that there are other concepts which belong to the understanding and are a prerequisite to fully grasp perceptions with understanding. Space and time are not objects of perception but they inform our perception of things. As space is not a perception derived from outer experiences, it must already exist in my understanding as a foundation for situating objects in relation to me and to each other. The concept is, therefore, like cause, a priori. Similarly, time is not drawn from perception. Neither co-existence nor succession would be perceived by us if the concept of time did not exist as a foundation, a priori. Kant identifies other concepts which are essential for the mind to grasp what the senses perceive. He called these Categories. There are twelve of them in four groups of three. One group he calls "Analogies of Experience."

Imagine you are looking at a forest. The sky is overcast, and little is visible between the trees. Suddenly, the sun breaks the clouds and you can now see clearly into the wood, flowers, fallen trees, a pathway, etc. Although the new image is very different from the previous one, you have no doubt the same underlying substance is there in both images. The concept of "substance" is an a priori condition for our experience.

The experience of a tulip requires not only awareness of its present shape, color, etc., but also the prior awareness of preceding stages which have brought about the present appearance. We grasp things in their coming-to-be, the causal chains to which everything is linked. Again, we have a construct of the mind which is prerequisite for taking hold of the world. Think of an object that has been discarded, or of an egg. Stop and look at a cloud. Awareness of succession in time is, therefore, an a priori condition for understanding the world.

A further example is the experience of a world of co-existing things that requires not only the experience of each thing individually but the presumption of their mutual interaction. A leaf throws its shadow on the bark of a tree. The shadow is moving. Sun, wind, leaf, and trunk coexist, making this event of mutual interaction "a community of experience."

The three examples are:

1. Principle of the permanence of substance.
2. Principle of the succession of time according to the law of causality.
3. Principle of co-existence according to the law of reciprocity or community.

These categories do not depend on sense perception and are, in Kant's language, transcendental. Having shown the transcendental means by which we take hold of the world of appearances, Kant wonders if the world is totally a creation of the mind. If the world we know is a construct of the mind, then what is the true world? To overcome this problem, Kant introduces the concept of "things-in-themselves" (*Dinge an sich selbst*). There is much divided opinion on how to understand this concept, but it is at least clear that Kant meant that there exist things which are unknowable, cannot be grasped by human understanding, and yet are real. This is a difficult notion but essential to Kant's picture of the universe. Let us look at the picture.

There are things-in-themselves.
We know nothing about things-in-themselves.

Kant also asserts:

Things-in-themselves are not in space and time.

But:

Things-in-themselves affect us causally.

Such statements have led to much discussion over the apparent contradictions. Kant has also introduced the concept of "noumenon" as distinct from phenomenon. Plato used noumenon to refer to things which can only be known to the intellect. Kant describes what he means as follows:

> I suppose (imagine) that there are things that are merely objects of the understanding and that, nevertheless, they can be given to an intuition, (grasped) though not to sensible intuition, (as sense perceptions are grasped) then such things can be called noumena.

What is this saying? Does it say that soul, self, questions of freedom and determinism, God and eternity belong to this world. The human being cannot not be excluded in the theory of how we understand the world or rather how the world comes to be understood by us. Morality is part of this world. Kant has found a place for them in the noumenal world. He seems to say that we can think of the noumenal as if it existed.

Reason itself requires us to suppose that we exist as substantial beings, that the world is meaningful, that free action is possible in a world ruled by cause and effect and that God exists. We cannot know these to be true, but that can in no way diminish the depth of our belief that they are. It appears that what were once metaphysical facts are now, with Kant, noumenal facts. He writes: "Only two things inspire genuine awe, the starry sky above and the moral within."

His view of morality asserts that actions are right according to the motives, and these motives are to be deduced from duty, not from inclination. Duty is the necessity to act out reverence for the law. So, the moral must be conceived so broadly, and so abstractly, that they encompass every possible set of circumstances. They have to be universal. Right actions are those that practical reason would "will" as universal law. This is Kant's categorical imperative: "Act in such a way that you treat humanity always as an end, and never simply as a means."

The question of morality cannot be separate from that of freedom. Kant as a strict disciple of Newton held that every event in nature resulted from a cause and took place in time. Human nature is no different from other realms of nature. Therefore, for a human action to be free, it must be outside both nature and time. Kant cannot accept those attempts to solve the problem by distinguishing between actions compelled by some event in the past and the capacity not to do the act in question. Instead, he offers the view that all of my intentional, voluntary actions are immediate effects of my noumenal self, which is causally undetermined. My noumenal self is an uncaused cause outside of time, which therefore is not subject to the deterministic laws of nature in accordance with which our understanding constructs experience. In this way, Kant hopes to escape from the restricting features of his predecessors.

Goethe was a contemporary of Kant and an admirer of his work. Although he is not numbered among the philosophers of his time, his genius was so great that it engaged with the deepest issues of the Age of Enlightenment to challenge its assumptions and accepted theories. In his scientific work, Goethe set up a challenge to the Newtonian method that will help us to see some of the obstacles which the philosophers failed to resolve.

Johann Wolfgang Goethe (1749 — 1832)

G oethe is recognized as the greatest poet, dramatist, and novelist of the German language. He was also a keen observer and engaged in scientific research, which he considered of equal, if not greater value than his literary output. His specific studies were on color, morphology in flowering plants, and the bone structure of animals.

Newton concluded from his experiments on prismatic colors that white light consisted of the range of colors so that each color was an element which, with all the other colors, made up white light. This was well known and accepted as a scientific truth. His experiment consisted in passing a beam of sunlight through a small aperture into a darkened room and through a glass prism and projected onto the wall. The image on the wall was oblong and not round like the aperture. It was lit with a spectrum of bright colors, what we know as the rainbow colors. In a further experiment Newton, made a second small aperture in a screen placed after the prism. He then selected one color only, which he then passed through a second prism. No further colors were formed by the second prism. He found that the angle through which the light was deviated by the second prism depended on the color. Newton had concluded that the colors were elements of white light, and each color could now be identified by its angle of deviation.

Goethe wanted to see for himself Newton's experiments and asked a friend to lend him his prisms. After a time, the friend asked Goethe to return his prisms. Goethe, who had not yet looked through them, quickly raised one to his eye and stared at a white wall. He was surprised that he saw no colors, yet white light was passing through the prism into his eye. He turned to the window with its bars and saw a range of colors. These appeared at the edge of the dark bars. For Goethe, this revealed that an encounter of the light with the dark was necessary for the appearance of colors, and, therefore, they could no longer be considered elements of white light. Goethe went on to make many experiments on colors, which eventually produced his *Theory of Colors* in 1810. Its importance for our philosophical story is in the challenge it presented to the scientific method of Galileo and his successors, who based science solely on what can be measured, weighed, or counted. It excludes all qualitative sense elements like color and sound, etc. It also challenged the mechanical theories of Descartes and Locke.

Goethe's method was to immerse himself in the experience of colors and stay within the experience. He rejected Newton's corpuscular theory of light and the temptation to explain color in terms of other elements external to the phenomena. In his search, he includes all aspects of color phenomena which can be observed in outer nature as well as in inner experience. He reflects on the qualities of colors. The "experience" of red is different from that of blue. Red is warm, blue cool. Red comes forward, blue withdraws. Red is loud, blue is quiet. Colors are thus linked with other senses, of warmth, of movement, of sound. He notes these observations not as subjective factors but as objective. He calls them "sensory-moral." Psychologists have made similar observations, but Goethe does not separate them from other color phenomena. He does not look for a theory from outside the phenomena. The theory is the phenomenon. He experiments on the effect of white light observed through a clouded medium. The light changes to yellow, then to red as the medium is darkened. If the medium is illuminated and a black background is viewed, then the black is lightened to blue. The phenomena of sun and sky are thus demonstrated. The worldview that emerges from this kind of investigation will be very different from the one which, according to Bacon, "tortures nature" to extract its secrets.

During his visit to Italy, Goethe had an inspiring insight into the nature of flowering plants. His insight or idea was his vision of the archetypal plant. Each plant is an example of the archetype. The different parts – leaf, petal, stamen, pistil – are transformations of leaf. Observation reveals in certain plants the leaf becoming a petal (tulip) or the petal form in the stamen. In this way nature reveals her secrets. This stands in contrast to the classification theory of Carl Linnaeus, the Swedish botanist, in which resemblances in plants are of prime importance.

Goethe's scientific method is an important contribution to our inquiry into the experience of thinking as revealed by different philosophers. The meditative insight which Goethe has brought to the understanding of Nature he expressed in verse:

> In the contemplation of nature, you must
> Regard the One as All;
> Nothing is within, nothing is without.
> Grasp that without delay
> A holy open secret.

A short historical interlude on the transition from the eighteenth century to the nineteenth will provide a helpful background to understand the philosophical questions that emerged in that period.

In 1776, the States of English settlers on the Eastern coast of America declared their independence from Britain. This was a deed full of hope for Europeans who argued for change in the political organization of society and in the abolition of the hereditary principle. Locke, Hume, and other philosophers had expressed these views. American independence was not just an idea but a deed. Democracy, religious freedom, freedom of expression, independence of the justice system. In the preamble to the Declaration of Independence, it is stated:

> We hold these truths to be self-evident that all
> men are created equal, that they are endowed by their
> Creator with certain inalienable rights that among
> these are Life, Liberty and the Pursuit of Happiness.
> That to secure these rights Governments are institut-
> ed among men deriving their just powers from the
> consent of the Governed.

One might argue that these principles were seriously undermined by the second amendment (1791), which strengthened the rights of states to maintain their militia whose main function was the control of slaves. Slavery was also a prominent issue amongst European nations at that time who were practicing their own forms of enslavement in their colonial possessions. Oblivious of this contradiction, in the nineteenth century, the USA was a magnet for the oppressed and the impoverished in Europe.

It certainly encouraged the French revolutionaries in 1789 when they stormed the Bastille and proclaimed the Rights of Man, even writing them in the blood that flowed from the guillotine in Paris. The revolutionaries also declared the threefold nature of the State with the words Liberty, Equality, and Fraternity. The Revolution eventually destroyed itself and from it emerged the enigmatic and extraordinary figure of Napoleon, military genius and lawmaker, who spread the ideals of the revolution through his conquests. For sixteen years, he was master of most of Europe in spite of his disastrous campaign in Russia and inability to compete with the British at sea.

This is also the period of the Romantic Movement, exemplified by composers and writers throughout Europe, such as Beethoven, Mozart, Novalis, Shelley, Coleridge, and Turner, to name but a few. Expressed in different ways was a sense of anticipation, of an awakening to new possibilities of the human spirit.

This is the world into which Hegel was born.

~

Georg Wilhelm Friedrich Hegel (1770 — 1831)

Hegel was born in Stuttgart, son of a minor official at the court of the Duke of Württemberg. As a schoolboy he was already familiar with classic Greek writers, Shakespeare, Goethe, and Schiller. He was enthusiastic about Spinoza and Kant. He kept his diary in Latin. When he was twenty-five, he wrote in appreciation of Kant's moral philosophy, "The philosophers are proving the dignity of man." He was professor in Jena, then Heidelberg and finally in Berlin.

In order to understand Hegel's philosophy, it will help us if we recall some of the ideas of Kant. He had explored the field of a priori synthetic statements, that is, statements the truth of which is verifiable independently of experience. He had identified causality, space, time, coexistence, and substance as independent of sense experience. These categories exist only as far as we apply them to the perceived world. In this way, Kant hoped to overcome the one-sidedness of rationalists and empiricists. It means that what we see is partly dependent on the structure of the mind. It also means that things in themselves are unknowable. In the following description, an imaginary physiological experience is described. This is an example to show how the mind is involved in understanding any visible observation:

> I am awake – lying more or less on my stomach – side and front of my face pressed into the pillow – eyes closed. Light appears – blurry white with thread-like white lines. It comes and goes. It changes to browny-red with straight geometric lines. This is a sensory experience in total darkness. I try to understand what is going on.
>
> I affirm that I am awake.
>
> The light is not in me. It seems to be out there. I have no special reference, so I try to locate it – perhaps two feet away but not sure.
>
> It goes on and off in a time experience.
>
> I am now using the categories space and time.

I look for a cause. Something must be causing it.

This is not an observation but a precondition to observation.

I compare it with other experiences of light. The mind tries, is it substance?

Light? – Bulb? – Phosphorescence?

The same I who is having this experience is having these memories.

Is this experience unique or are there other examples? How does it compare with other sense experiences like touch, pain?

A provisional thought: the light is produced by pressure on the eyeball making it appear in the dark.

The knowledge acquired depends on a sense experience plus the mental activity represented by the categories. In this case space, time and cause.

This typifies a Kantian approach to cognition. Structures of the mind enable us to grasp what the senses give us, but does not give us any sure knowledge of the thing in itself. Kant had opened a vast new field of inquiry. His world is split between the world we can know and study and the world that exists 'In itself' but is unknowable.

Johann Gottlieb Fichte (1762–1814) was the first to attempt to overcome the problem of the split. Like Descartes, he starts with one's own self-consciousness as the one thing we are sure of. By examining the act of thought, he arrived at his first three principles. The first is that the ego is present in every act of knowing. It is infinite and inexhaustible in nature, but one only knows it in its activity, which is to give attention. Second, this gives rise to the object. The object is outside the self, part of the non-self. Third, the ego and object interact. Finally, the ego understands and unites with the object. In describing an object, for example, a dialogue is going on between I and an event in the world. Out of this dialogue, something new has arisen. It is not that I have just acquired some knowledge for myself. The concept evolved goes beyond the self; it changes the self and makes the object what it is. Something new has come about.

Fichte provides a helpful preliminary to Hegel, whose first major work is called *Phenomenology of Spirit*. The title is also translated *Philosophy of Mind*. "Geist" means both Spirit and Mind, and different translators make their choice. They have different meanings and the choice determines the translator's meaning. In English, mind suggests an activity and spirit more a state. With Hegel the spirit is active.

At the beginning of *Phenomenology*, Hegel observes that Locke and Kant considered cognition as a kind of instrument or tool enabling us to grasp the world out there and come to know it. Or else they saw cognition as a medium through which the world can be assimilated by us. Such philosophers are, for Hegel, on the wrong track. The proper approach is to put aside all presuppositions and begin a systematic investigation of knowledge as a "phenomenon." Hegel also objects to the distinction of the Absolute from cognition. Absolute is an important concept for Hegel. It embodies the idea of Spirit which is active in the universe. Cognition, the act of thinking, is not a separate activity. He rejects the common notion that thinking is limited to what goes on in the heads of humans, a unique event found nowhere else in the universe.

Hegel also confronts the accepted view of the split between man and nature. According to this view, on the one side was nature, essentially inert and lifeless (animals were considered like machines obeying certain prescribed laws) and on the other side the human being able to act out of themselves, to reflect on their actions, to create and have values, to cognize the universe, to set ends for themselves, to find meaning or not. The task of philosophy was, for Hegel, to find a bridge over this gulf.

The nominalists had reduced the concept to a label. To move forward, Hegel would restore it to its full significance.

The concept is the very heart of all things and makes them what they are. To form the concept of an object means therefore to become aware of its concept, and when we go on to criticize or judge an object, we are not making a subjective act ascribing this or that predicate (value or significance) to the object. On the contrary, we are observing the object in the specific character imposed by the concept.

Thoughts are not just the product of the human mind but permeate the world and constitute the substance of external things. Hegel holds that the concept is an organizing principle; it melds the material out of which it is made into a coherent structure. The thought, which arises in the human being, has its counterpart as thought-form in the objects of nature. When a boat-builder builds a boat, his thought-through design gets embodied in the boat. So, in the rose there is embodied the concept of rose. With the boat, the concept is imposed from the outside. With the rose, it is the organizing principle within.

Hegel, in one of his later works, *Encyclopedia*, points to what he regards as the main characteristics of metaphysics, namely, that the true nature of things is knowable through thought alone. His method was sometimes described as dialectical, consisting of three stages: thesis, antithesis, synthesis. Hegel never used these terms – in fact, he criticized them. Hegel's most usual terms were: Abstract, Negative, Concrete. According to Professor Walter Kaufman:

The formula, thesis-antithesis-synthesis, does not explain why the thesis requires an antithesis. However, the formula, abstract-negative-concrete, suggests a flaw, or perhaps an incompleteness, in any initial thesis – it is too abstract and lacks the negative of trial, error, and experience. For Hegel, the concrete, the synthesis, the absolute, must always pass through the phase of the negative, in the journey to completion, that is, mediation. This is the essence of what is popularly called Hegelian dialectics.

To describe the activity of overcoming the negative, Hegel often used the term *Aufhebung* (overcoming), to conceive of the working of the dialectic. Roughly, the term indicates preserving the useful portion of an idea, thing, society, etc., while moving beyond its limitations. In his *Logic*, Hegel describes a dialectic of existence:

> First, existence must be posited as pure Being (*Sein*); but pure Being, upon examination, is found to be indistinguishable from Nothing (*Nichts*). When it is realized that what is coming into being is, at the same time, also returning to nothing (in life, for example, one's living is also a dying), both Being and Nothing are united as Becoming.
>
> For example: Life – Death – Becoming

This line of reasoning raises many problems in contemporary culture. I shall leave it to our next philosopher, Kierkegaard, to respond to its implications. For Hegel, the diversity of philosophies is a positive indication of the progressive unfolding of the truth. It is not valuable just to focus on their disagreements. Philosophy has to become a science, an inquiry to establish the truth, not just a love of philosophical discourse. The endeavors of Descartes and other philosophers to start from a base on which truth can be built and falsehood identified is not Hegel's way: "A principle or basic proposition is both true and false because it is only the beginning, it is not actual knowledge. The refutation cannot be made externally but by the development of the proposition."

The world presents us with many negative examples in morality, in knowledge, and in aesthetics. The dialectical method does not shun their presence but involves them in the process of advancing to "absolute knowing," which I take to indicate an understanding which transcends what other philosophers have attempted and which is called "spirit." "Absolute" and "spiritual" are equivalents.

As an example of Hegel's relevance to everyday life, I quote from a letter which C. L. R. James wrote to a friend in 1943.

> Why the popularity of Westerns? Because young people who sit cramped up in buses and tied to assembly lines terribly wish they could be elsewhere.... Like all art, but more than most, movies are not merely a reflection, but an extension of the actual – an extension along the lines which people feel are lacking and possible in the actual. That, my dear, is the complete secret of Hegelian dialectic. The two, the actual and the potential are always inseparably linked, one is always giving way to the other. At a certain stage, a crisis takes place and a complete change is the result.

Hegel's *Philosophy of History* presents the great civilizations from China, India, and the succession of civilizations in the Near East as an evolutionary path of the human spirit. Greek culture manifests a specific moment in the awakening to the nature of Reason ("nous" in the Greek of Anaxagoras and subsequent thinkers).

Hegel distinguishes three modes of doing history: Original History, Reflective History, and Philosophical History. Original history is like that of Thucydides or Tacitus. These are almost contemporaneous writings limited to deeds, events, and states of society which they had before their very eyes and whose culture they shared. Reflective history is written at some distance in time from the period considered. However, for Hegel, this form of history has a tendency to impose the cultural prejudices and ideas of the historians' era upon the past history over which the historian reflects. Philosophical history, for Hegel, is the true way. Hegel maintains that with philosophical history, the historian must bracket his own preconceptions and go and find the overall sense and the driving ideas out of the very matter of the history considered.

Hegel's *Philosophy of History* describes an evolution in which divine providence is reconciled with evil. He considers the events of history to be governed by universal reason:

> That world history is governed by an ultimate design, that it is a rational process ... this is a proposition whose truth we must assume; its proof lies in the study of world history itself, which is the image and enactment of reason.

Hegel writes, "History is not the soil in which happiness grows. The periods of happiness in it are the blank pages of history." And further:

> We must first of all know what the ultimate design of the world really is, and secondly, we must see that this design has been realized and that evil has not been able to maintain a position of equality beside it. To see the reason in history is to be able to account for the evil within it.
>
> We must first note that the object we have before us, world history, belongs to the realm of the spirit. The nature of spirit can be best understood with its direct opposite, matter. Just as gravity is the substance of matter, freedom is the substance of spirit. It is immediately obvious to everyone that freedom is one of the attributes of spirit, but philosophy teaches us that all the attributes of spirit exist only by virtue of freedom.

Freedom is a principal ideal of the Romantic Movement. It stimulated national liberation movements to demand freedom of expression and of the press and the right of the individual to live his or her own life.

Hegel's concept of freedom as the essence of spiritual striving appealed to the Romantic mood, although not always understood.

In the *Philosophy of Right*, Hegel distinguishes between abstract freedom and real freedom. Abstract freedom is doing what one wants to do and real freedom is acting out of a spiritual understanding, which is not driven by personal aims or social pressures.

The following event gives us a glimpse of Hegel which may reveal an aspect of his concept of freedom.

Because the city of Jena was occupied by French troops under Napoleon in 1806, Hegel was forced to leave the city. But he did witness Napoleon's entry into the city and, as an admirer of the French Revolution, was delighted to witness first-hand this "world spirit on horseback" passing by.

Two thinkers challenge the idealism of Hegel, and their reaction will have a strong influence on philosophy and politics in the twentieth century – Kierkegaard and Karl Marx. The first will oppose the way spirit and reason are presented and the second will subvert them and make the foundations material, not spiritual.

Søren Kierkegaard (1813 — 1855)

The strongest reaction to Hegel's philosophy came from a surprising quarter. Søren Kierkegaard, a Danish writer in Copenhagen published *Either/Or* under the pseudonym Victor Eremita (Latin for "victorious hermit"). Kierkegaard, who had finished his degree in theology, was already known as the writer of a critical study of Hans Andersen's tales. After breaking an engagement with a young lady, as he felt that marriage was not for him, he devoted a year to writing the lengthy "letter," as he called it, (over 700 pages) *Either/Or*. It is a search, on one hand, to find his life-view and also to demolish the kind of impersonal system of Hegel's which ignores the lived experience of human beings.

The book describes two kinds of personalities, the aesthetic and the ethical. Aesthetic normally is applied to the appreciation of painting and other arts, but it also applies to our everyday experience. The aesthetic type looks for special moments, which give life its richness. The term covers different forms visible in social life and is especially found in Romanticism. The lover dreams of the loved one. Obstacles have to be overcome. Finally, the magical union is achieved. End of story. There is no place for the rest of life. It is complete in the moment. The aesthetic is open to what life provides. Immediacy is what binds all kinds of aesthetics. They are awake to the moment. They don't choose. It is as if the moment chooses him. If one just looks for pleasure, it is often disappointing. It is best when it arrives out of the blue. The other personality is the ethical. This does not mean conventional morality. Its essence is the act of choice. The aesthetic just goes through life hoping for pleasure, looking for moments (a lottery win?). The ethical chooses: Shall I become an artist or a businessman? In the former, they will probably be poor and raising a family will be hard; in the latter, life will be easy and pleasant but it is art, which is really their desire.

Choosing solidifies the personality, says Kierkegaard. It is possible that the decision is made without choosing. A parent decides. An opportunity is missed. A bad choice is better than no choice. On the result, another choice can present itself. It is not so much a question of choosing the right, as of the energy, the earnestness, the pathos with which one chooses. Thereby, the personality announces its inner infinity. The aesthetical in a human being is that by which they are immediately what they are; the ethical is that whereby they becomes what they become.

There is only one situation in which the choice is absolute; in questions of truth, righteousness, and holiness. For these there is no 'Or."

> For freedom, therefore, I am fighting (partly in
> this letter and principally within myself). This treasure is deposited in thine own inner self; there is an
> either/or which makes a man greater than the angels.

Hegel's dialectics was a clear target for Kierkegaard. Fundamentally, the idea that Hegel's system, as he saw it, could explain the whole of reality was offensive to him. Any system implying completeness must be false because reality and human beings are incomplete. Kierkegaard sees Hegel's work in the following manner.

The creation of the universe is presented as the original dialectical process. God, that is Being, stands opposed to Nothing and from this tension the third event, Becoming, arises. Satan, the angel who has fallen away, is the middle term and represents the divine who has become self-alienated. Such triads permeate the whole of reality. Since the human mind is merely a manifestation of the divine mind, the crisis of the godhead is repeated in the human. Hegel expresses the three stages as 'unreflective unity," 'reflective disunity," and 'reflective unity." It is present in history in the encounter of opposing elements, which eventually through conflict give birth to a new culture.

Such a view of history ignores the experience of individuals and communities in the process of change. If change is the product of dialectical forces, then human freedom, human ethics, and human engagement are eliminated. Personalities who are engaged in changing society through ideas and action are like pawns in Hegel's system. Periods that seem to be in regression are made to fit the dialectic by the Cunning of Reason. Dialectics requires the recognition of the opposite, the contradictory in order that the third stage can emerge. Kierkegaard expresses the dialectic as the "Both/And." Hence the "Either/Or."

Hegel regarded the State as an independent entity more important than any individual. It had its own evolution to accomplish in which the human being had no part. Kierkegaard regarded this as dehumanizing and Hegel's concept of freedom as illusory.

Hegel described the first stage of the child as "unreflective unity," which in the rebellious teenager is confronted by the "reflective disunity" stage. Finally, in adulthood the "reflective unity" is attained. The disunity is resolved in reconciliation. Not so, Kierkegaard would reply, reconciliation would mean a return to submission. The adult has to manage a "tenuous holding together of the self" between two opposing forces, the desire for union with parents and the need to maintain an independent self.

At this point, we might consider the particular use Kierkegard makes of various pseudonyms he adopts for his writings. On the title page of *Either/Or* is the name Victor Eremita. I have been referring in my quotations to "Kierkegaard," knowing the pseudonym is fictional like Mary Ann Evans signing her novels "George Eliot." The difference is that people knew it was Kierkegaard who wrote the book, so he was not hiding anything. He himself explains that although he wrote the book, it was not to express his thoughts but the thoughts of another. If he signed the book, he would be classified as anti-Hegelian and thus entangled in a process he aims to avoid. The book, therefore, is describing the ordinary attitudes of the multitude that are mostly living for the immediate. He wants to put up a mirror in which the populace can see itself. To argue with another's beliefs is a waste of time. He (Kierkegaard) also warns against the view that the Ethical is a subsequent stage to the aesthetical. If anything, they are simultaneous. In the list of his publications, most are pseudonymous. Those directly dealing with religion are in the writer's name.

This, for me, raises wider questions, wider than the effort to understand this philosopher's philosophy. He does not aim to persuade his readers to understand and accept his truth but to motivate them to find their truth: "All communication of knowledge is direct communication. All communication of capability is indirect communication."

He avoids challenging and instead goes along with the other's delusion. His battle was not with objective theories, which could be proved wrong, but with various "styles of living," which were both subjective truths and also illusions: "An illusion can never be destroyed directly, but only by indirect means can it be radically removed."

His method requires an imaginative approach, which will vary with each person. He uses irony and humor as tools to undermine a stubborn opponent. He takes his cue from Socrates in the case of irony. For example, Socrates regularly asserts his own ignorance. When told that the Delphic Oracle had named him the wisest man in Athens, he pretended to be shocked and then admitted that he was wiser than others because he knew nothing and knew he knew nothing; others also knew nothing but thought they knew something. The ironic perspective on life is a step in separating oneself from the world around. It thus asserts one as an independent individual.

The parables of Jesus given in the gospels are also a model for Kierkegaard: "Men are mostly subjective towards themselves and objective towards others, but the task is the opposite; to be objective towards oneself and subjective towards all others."

Ironic detachment is only a stage in a process. If it becomes a permanent way of life, it can lead to despair. The task is "the awakening of subjectivity."

What Kierkegaard calls subjective truth is, for him, the highest truth available for humankind. This does not mean that one holds certain beliefs, which are separable from oneself, but that one lives within subjective truth. The process of existing is the exploring and discovering of one's subjectivity. Objective statements about the world remain so until they are amended or rejected. They do not reach into the inner experience. "The inward deepening in and through existing is truth."

Kierkegaard's father was born into a hard life as a serf owned by a rural church. While tending the sheep in a harsh landscape, he climbed a rock and solemnly cursed God. When serfs were liberated, he was apprenticed to work in the textile trade and eventually became a successful businessman moving in comfortable social circles. After the death of his wife, he married the servant who was illiterate. In spite of his worldly success, the father was burdened with a deep sense of guilt and believed that God would punish him. Of his seven children, only Søren and his brother survived. The father was a harsh disciplinarian and also an unusual teacher of his son in whom he recognized unusual abilities. Not allowed to go out, Søren was, instead, taken on an imaginary walk through the streets of Copenhagen. The father described everything they saw in immense detail, which the son had to recall, and, afterwards, was as exhausted as if he had made a real walk. Religious guilt and stern reproaches were part of his upbringing. Later he spent a life of "dissipation" apparently enjoying the superficial pleasures of a dandy. Kierkegaard's life and work are especially interwoven; hence, I note these brief biographical facts.

Kierkegaard's work *Fear and Trembling* was published not long after *Either/Or*. He writes under the name Johannes de Silentio, which is the name of the servant in one of Grimm's fairy tales. The servant has the power to bring back to life the three children murdered by his master.

The central theme in the book is the story of Abraham's sacrifice of his son Isaac. It raises enigmatic questions. God tells Abraham to prepare to journey to a mountain with his son Isaac and on arriving there after three days, to build an altar and sacrifice his son. Abraham obeys, and as he raises the knife, Isaac is replaced by a ram. This illustrates Abraham's faith. The translator of *Fear and Trembling* has inserted Bob Dylan's song, which gives a normal reaction to the story.

God said to Abraham, "Kill me a son"
Abe say, "Man, you must be puttin' me on"
God say, "No," Abe say, "What?"
God say, "You can do what you want Abe, but
Next time you see me comin', you better run"
Abe said, "Where do you want this killin' done?"
God said, "Out on Highway 61"

From a modern perspective, it is easy to see God as a tyrant submitting his believer to his irrational will. Yet for Christians, Abraham is the figure who guided his people and taught them the true reality of the one God. He is the supreme example of faith. Contemporary Christians were content to ignore the contradiction of an act of faith and an act of murder.

The content of the book is a subtle and complex investigation of a story that belongs to the three religions that honor Abraham as their founder, Jewish, Christian, and Muslim. Each finds its unique meaning in different ways. The challenge is for the committed Christian to understand the meaning of faith as represented by the story.

For Hegel, it can only be a remnant from a period when truths were shown in picture language, and now this approach is superseded by an objective grasp of the ideas that make possible their understanding. All moral systems, whether Hegelian or Kantian, must repudiate the story. For them, God is Reason incarnate, so any judgment on the basis of Reason is beyond questioning. *Fear and Trembling* is Kierkegaard's way to undermine this, to provide a theological shock treatment to awaken readers to the huge demands of faith.

The writer, Johannes, in trying to fathom faith and the act of sacrifice, supposes two reactions by Abraham to the command by God. One is resignation and the other is faith. Johannes does not claim to be either a philosopher or a Christian. He is both attracted and repelled by the story. His rational mind finds faith incomprehensible and cries out in despair, "Abraham, I cannot understand."

He imagines two figures that will be able to help him: the knight of infinite resignation and the knight of infinite faith. The first, in obedience to God's call, has given up his dearest worldly hope, the son given to him by God to be his successor, and is completely convinced of the impossibility of regaining life as it was before. The knight of infinite faith also has the same conviction, but in addition, he knows that life as before will return as God will restore his son to him. Such an expectation is absurd, being humanly impossible. This knight, therefore, is able to believe with certainty that the whole deed of sacrifice and restoration will come about even when proved humanly impossible. The knight of resignation, having given his son to God will now focus on his love for God and withdraw from earthly attachments. This total renunciation without faith in obedience to God is possible with enough will but reduces the individual to a total dependence and nothingness in the face of the divine.

There is a double movement in the case of the knight of infinite faith. He also resigns himself to God's will but at the same time, he embraces infinite faith. For Johannes, these two movements are at the same moment and also mutually exclusive. One might suppose that the story is just a test of Abraham's faith. God did not intend Isaac's death. The ram was backstage to be brought on when Abraham had proved himself! Such a supposition shows how little the understanding of faith is. The average Christian thinks that one starts with faith and one moves on. There is no realization of the huge dimension of faith, which is a goal one is forever striving towards.

Johannes proceeds to extract from Abraham's story its dialectical element, in the form of *Problemata*, in order to see what a monstrous paradox faith is, a paradox capable of making a murder into a holy act well pleasing to God, a paradox which gives Isaac back to Abraham, which no thought can grasp because faith begins precisely where thinking leaves off.

Problema I deals with the statement that the ethical is universal. If so, there are no exceptions to the moral rules, and they apply to everyone.

Faith is just this paradox that the single individual, as the particular, is higher than the universal. This is justified, though in such a way that having been in the universal, the single individual now sets themselves as the particular above the universal. This paradox must remain for all eternity.

Problema II. This questions whether there is an absolute to God. In Hegelian terms, the outer is higher than the inner, therefore, God is absolute. For Johannes, faith is this paradox that interiority is higher than exteriority. Abraham as the knight of faith, having passed through resignation, responds directly to God. Johannes compares Abraham and the knight of faith with the tragic hero in an amazing passage. The tragic hero renounces himself in order to express the universal; the knight of faith renounces the universal in order to be the particular. The hero has his place in the world of universals and the path to his fate is like a dance compared to the slow, uncomprehending journey of the knight of faith. Fear and trembling accompany him. However, writes Johannes, he addresses God in heaven as "Thou."

Problema III. Was it ethical of Abraham to conceal his purpose from Sarah and Isaac?

Abraham, isolated from the universal, is unable to explain or reveal his actions.

Johannes concludes by pointing out that faith requires passion, and passion is not something we can learn. We have to experience it ourselves, or else we do not understand it at all.

After his death, the writings of Kierkegaard were ignored and largely forgotten until the twentieth century when they reemerged carrying a very contemporary message.

Karl Marx (1818 — 1883)

"Philosophers have only interpreted the world, the point is to change it."

Marx's reaction to Hegel's work is of a very different order from that of Kierkegaard. He did not criticize it, he subverted it.

Hegel describes the world process as the progressive evolution of Reason, Marx makes the process a material, economic one to transform society and social relations.

Marx was born in Trier in the Rhineland into a Jewish family. His father had converted to Christianity to enable him to practice as a lawyer. After achieving his doctorate and being unable to get an academic appointment, Marx turned to journalism and radical politics. He moved to London and lived there in poverty in Soho. While in Germany, he had met Friedrich Engels, son of a very prosperous businessman, who shared his radical views and had published articles in magazines edited by Marx. In one, Engels revealed what he regarded as the contradictions in liberal economic doctrine and set out to prove that the existing system based on private property was leading to a world of "millionaires and paupers." "The revolution that would follow would lead to the elimination of private property and the reconciliation of humanity with nature and itself."

In 1844 Engels' father arranged for his son to work with his firm in Manchester. Engels was appalled at the working conditions he observed in the factories and published his findings in *The Conditions of the Working Class* in England. In 1848 Marx and Engels published the *Communist Manifesto*. In it religion is analyzed in detail and described as the "opium of the people." According to the Manifesto, material existence creates religion. The working class is alienated by the conditions it has to endure, and out of their need to express their communal essence, workers take up religion, which it hopes will fulfill it.

The question of how revolution in Germany might be achieved is also set out in the book, which examines the role of the proletariat in bringing about the emancipation of society as a whole. In 1848 Germany was divided into several states, large and small, of which Prussia was the largest and the dominant.

The theme of alienation and the alienation of the working class is not, for Marx, a subjective reaction to certain conditions. The alienated worker is the plaything of alien forces and these are the product of human action. In our daily lives we take decisions that have unintended consequences which then combine to create large-scale social forces which may have utterly unpredicted effects. Institutions of capitalism – consequences of human behavior – structure our future behavior, determining the possibilities of our action. The business man in a capitalist society is bound to exploit the worker because that is the system.

Marx's theory of history is of a process which furthers or hinders the development of human productive power. The process moves through a series of modes of economic production, culminating in the overthrow of bourgeois society.

Marx described his research on the conditions of the working class in England at the time in the first volume of his major work, *Das Kapital*, published in 1867. Although the exploitation of children and women was no longer so severe as in the 1830s and 1840s, and working conditions had improved, all the injustices of the economic system were visible. The wage earner as slave to the market and labor as a commodity were not to disappear. Marx did much of his research in the British library, which held extensive collections of books and documents, providing social and economic information not only on England but on colonial territories as well. He was able to show the disastrous consequences for the Indian peasant when the British introduced the practice of mortgaging land. The peasant could now be reduced to slavery. The second and third volumes of *Das Kapital* were published by Engels after the death of Marx. They contain his analysis of capitalism, its inherent contradictions and inevitable collapse. The consequence of Marx's theory is a large part of the history of the twentieth century and is outside our task.

John Stuart Mill (1806 — 1873)

M ill was the outstanding thinker and social reformer in nineteenth-century Britain. His early life and education were extraordinary. His father, James Mill, was a social reformer and close friend of Jeremy Bentham, founder of Utilitarianism. This is a philosophy of moral action, which became an important influence in Victorian England. James Mill undertook the education of his son so that he would be able to promote these ideas when he grew up. He therefore began his education early. The son was extremely precocious. At three, he was taught Greek, at eight he had read Aesop, Xenophon, the whole of Herodotus, and was acquainted with six dialogues of Plato. He was also taught Latin, mathematics, physics, and astronomy. At ten, he could read Latin and Greek with ease. His father also included the study and composing of poetry. At twelve, he was studying scholastic logic and Aristotle's logic. The following year, he was studying the political economy of Adam Smith. During a year in France, the prodigy was able to meet and converse with notable intellectuals. When he was twenty, he went through a deep depression, which he attributed to the rigorous intellectual demands made during his early childhood. He was helped to recover by the poetry of William Wordsworth, which showed him that beauty generates compassion for others and stimulates joy.

He was unable to get a place at Oxford or Cambridge Universities, as he would not sign the 39 articles, which define the doctrine of the Anglican Church. Instead, he joined the East India Trading Company, which more or less ruled India until it was taken over by the British Crown in 1856. Mill also proposed reforms, which were well ahead of his time. He was an advocate of women's rights. He had met Harriet Taylor, a remarkable woman who became a significant influence in his life. For twenty-one years, they had a close relationship, and after the death of her husband, they married. Mill wrote that she was the author on women's rights in *The Subjection of Women* and he was the amanuensis. Mill also favored labor unions, farm cooperatives, the extension of the suffrage, and advanced proposals for proportional representation and the single transferable vote.

Mill sets out his philosophy in his two essays: *On Liberty* and *Utilitarianism*. What is liberty and what are its limits in a modern society? What power can the state legitimately exercise over its citizens? Mill asserts, 'the only purpose for which power can be rightfully exercised over any member of a civilized community, against his will, is to prevent harm to others," with the exception of those incapable of self-government, such as children, and those living in backward states of society. Mill goes on to examine exactly what is meant by 'harm" and what are exceptions.

He sees the struggle between Liberty and Authority as a conspicuous feature in history. Liberty was a contest between subjects and government. In contemporary society, liberty was about the protection of society from the tyranny of political rulers. Tyranny can also take the form of the tyranny of the majority. These required limitations on the power of the ruler to prevent power being used in the interests of the ruler. People must have a say in how they are governed. There must be certain rights, which are recognized as inalienable. Constitutional checks must also be available to rein in the government. Limiting the power of government, however, was not enough. In many areas, society governs itself, and if it makes mistakes, it can amend these. However, if the government meddles in such matters, it becomes a tyrant more formidable than many kinds of political oppression since it is difficult to oppose and is able to penetrate much more deeply into life, enslaving the soul itself.

The despotism of custom is everywhere the outstanding hindrance to human advancement. There is a never-ending struggle to oppose that kind of tyranny in order to cultivate something better than what is customary. This is called, according to circumstances, the spirit of liberty, the march of progress or improvement.

Mill was a passionate defender of freedom of speech as a necessary condition for intellectual and social progress. Permitting people to air false opinions is an opportunity to combat them and possibly change them. It can also challenge dogma, which thrives in an unfree society. In many ways, Mill anticipated liberal views common today. Freedom of speech was a vital way to develop talents and realize a person's potential and creativity. He writes against religious intolerance, slavery, (when he wrote, slavery still existed in the USA), colonialism, racial inequality, and advocated voting rights for women (granted in UK in 1919).

Utilitarianism founded by social reformer Jeremy Bentham, was the life project of J S Mill. He defined it as the greatest happiness principle.

> Actions are right in proportion, as they tend to promote happiness, wrong, as they tend to produce the reverse of happiness. By happiness is intended pleasure, and the absence of pain; by unhappiness, pain, and the privation of pleasure. Pleasures have different qualities. What makes one more valuable than another?

Mill answers the question as follows:

> Of two pleasures, if there be one to whom all or most of all have experience of both give a decided preference, irrespective of any feeling of moral obligation to prefer it, that is the more desirable pleasure.

The happiness principle is based not primarily on the individual but mainly on the community. Mill believed that for the majority of people (those with but a moderate degree of sensibility and of capacity for enjoyment) happiness is best achieved en passant, rather than striving for it directly. This meant no self-consciousness, scrutiny, self-interrogation, dwelling on, thinking about, imagining or questioning one's happiness.

> Then, if otherwise fortunately circumstanced, one would inhale happiness with the air you breathe. Nature is not a machine to be built after a model,

and set to do exactly the work prescribed for it, but a tree, which requires to grow and develop itself on all sides, according to the tendency of the inward forces, which make it a living thing.

Mill maintained that people have a "strong utilitarian conscience (i.e., a strong feeling of obligation to the general happiness)," a desire to be happy, and that desire causes us to want to be in unity with other humans, to care about the happiness of others, as well as the happiness of complete strangers. But this desire also causes us to experience pain when we perceive harm to other people. Internal sanctions make us experience guilt and induce appropriate actions. These internal sanctions make us want to do good because we do not want to feel guilty for our actions. Happiness is our ultimate end because it is our duty. He argues that we do not need to be constantly motivated by the concern of people's happiness because most of the actions done by people are done out of good intention, and the good of the world is made up of the good of the people.

That gives a summary of the content of Mill's social philosophy, of utilitarianism. It cannot be proved by reasoning. The only proof that something brings one pleasure is if someone finds it pleasurable. Morality is the basic way to achieve happiness and moral rules refer to the furtherance of individual and general happiness. The notion of utility relates to the human being as a progressive being developing rational capacities to achieve a higher mode of existence.

Finally, Mill redefines happiness in the following way: "The ultimate end, for the sake of which all other things are desirable (whether we are considering our own good or that of other people) is an existence as free as possible from pain and as rich as possible in enjoyments."

Friedrich Nietzsche (1844 — 1900)

Nietzsche was repelled by the bourgeois complacency of the nineteenth century and had a strong intuition of what was coming. Since his death, his work has been much misrepresented. Now the history of the twentieth century has justified his premonitions.

He is known for the statement, "God is dead," in his most famous book, *Thus Spake Zarathustra*. In an earlier book called *The Gay Science* (die fröhliche Wissenschaft), a madman shouts, "God is dead. We have killed him." The title of the book includes the subtitle *'la gaya scienza"* which derives from *gai saber*, a poetic academy founded in Provence in the thirteenth century, which Nietzsche admired so much. For them the phrase meant joyfulness and passion in the crafts of poetry and knowledge.

How has God been killed? Religion and metaphysics in the nineteenth century still claimed that they referred to a reality, but it was a hollow pretense. The power of the scientific method and the promise and success of technology seemed to have no boundaries and claimed to be relevant to all aspects of the, as yet, unexplored universe and human being. Metaphysical inquiry and religious beliefs were now defunct as the source of moral and aesthetic values. From what source could these now be engendered?

Nietzsche foresaw a Europe lacking the guidance which had existed through past centuries. The philistine, the mediocre, a slavish mentality, a rejection of all higher spiritual values would rule the day. He also foresaw a century of great wars and conflicts. He saw this coming at a time when leading nations like Victorian Britain and Bismarck Germany were dreaming of peace through dominance and undiminished supremacy in trade, technology, and military power. Little did they know!

Nietzsche's father was a pastor and teacher in the Lutheran church in the Electorate of Saxony. He died after suffering for a year from a brain tumor when his son was eight. His brother also died that year – events which weighed heavily on the young Nietzsche. He was an outstanding scholar and decided to study theology at university. After an inner crisis, which he described to his sister, he refused to attend Easter Mass. He was no longer able to accept the Christian doctrine. He changed his study to classical philology and at the unusually early age of twenty-four was appointed professor of philology at Basel University.

To replace the void left by the abandonment of religion, he turned to art, especially music. He was deeply influenced by the philosopher Arthur Schopenhauer (1788–1860) whose pessimistic view of life appealed to his mood of increasing hostility to the prevalent complacency in bourgeois Germany. In his thinking, Schopenhauer developed hostility to life and a belief that one could meditate about reality only if one escaped from that reality. The noise of the world disturbed his thoughts. A temporary flight from the world may help a deeper understanding but the flight must not become the aim. Nietzsche identified with this ascetic approach.

Nietzsche also fell under the spell of Richard Wagner who was at the height of his career. Both were living in Switzerland and able to meet regularly. Wagner's music and his study of Greek art inspired him to write his first book *The Birth of Tragedy* at the age of twenty-eight. Sixteen years later, he composed an *Attempt at Self-Criticism*, which he included in a later publication. This gives an insight into Nietzsche's mentality and also celebrates a rejection of Wagner's music and influence.

In *The Birth of Tragedy*, Nietzsche describes two tendencies present in Greek art, which he calls the Apollonian and the Dionysian. The god Apollo presides over the art of sculpture and partly also poetry; the god Dionysus is the inspirer of music. The first is the world of the dream, the second of intoxication. These are artistic energies, which burst out from nature herself without the mediation of the human artist. The completeness of the image world of art is not dependent on the intellectual attitude or artistic culture of an individual. Likewise, the intoxicated reality of the Dionysian does not heed the individual; it even seeks to destroy him and redeem him by a mystic feeling of oneness. A statue by Polyclitus and the poems of Homer in their clarity and beauty are Apollonian. Apollo was the sun god. The bacchanalian festivals led by Silenus and his satyrs are under the intoxicating influence of Dionysus.

A little-known poet Archilochus, whose life in the seventh century BC was tragic and turbulent, was opposed to Homer and was founder of the folk song and lyric poetry. Such was the beginning, according to Nietzsche, of the objective and subjective in art. The opposites of thought and will also characterize the two worlds. In the Greek tragedies of Aeschylus and Sophocles, the chorus represents the Dionysian. The dithyrambic chorus was a wild and impassioned hymn addressed to the god Dionysus. The tragic suffering, which is so strongly represented in Greek theatre in the fate of Oedipus, for example, is triumphed over finally. This overcoming of the impossible, of what reason cannot explain or achieve, is owed to the magical destroyer of barriers, which is the Dionysian. Nietzsche quotes a short poem by Goethe, as illustration of this will to overcome. Prometheus is the god who out of his suffering brought fire to humanity.

> Here I sit, forming men in my own image
> a race to be like me
> to suffer, to weep
> to delight and to rejoice
> and to defy you as I do.

Although Nietzsche was later highly critical of *The Birth of Tragedy,* it introduces us to a mind which searches beyond the truths acquired by the rational and analytical formulations. In the article of self-criticism cited above, this son of a pastor shows his fierce antipathy to Christianity, which teaches a morality that is hostile to life. He is no atheist like Hume or Mill. Christianity, however, is a religion, which removes all care of the earthly from man. It is the religion of the weak. The Kingdom of God spoils the capacity to see the real world. Advanced Christians, he observed, no longer believe in the resurrection and eternal life in paradise or hell. They believe in divine providence and that human being must raise themselves above terrestrial goals and adapt to an ideal realm. The Dionysian he describes as the antithesis of that; the Dionysian is the Antichrist. While Nietzsche was virulent in his condemnation of Christianity, its followers, and especially its priests, he was capable of deep compassion, as we shall see below. I shall deal later with the question of his scorn expressed in the virulent language against Christianity, Christians, and especially its priests.

Later in his book *Ecce Homo,* he writes about his discovery of the wonderful phenomenon of the Dionysian.

> At the same time, my discovery that Socrates was a decadent proved how little the sureness of my psychological grasp would be endangered by any moral idiosyncrasy; seeing morality itself as a symptom of decadence...my discovery is an innovation of the first rank in the history of knowledge.

For me, his condemnation of Socrates is due to the conviction that life's problems are not met by asking: What is this, what is that? Nietzsche admired the Greek virtue of cheerfulness. Life was precious and the afterlife dismal. "Better be a beggar in the land of the living than a king in the land of the dead," as Odysseus discovered, when, in his travels, he descended to the underworld.

In *Thus Spake Zarathustra,* Nietzsche changes from devastating critic to teacher and poet. This work is not easily summarized or condensed. His teaching is a hammer, which has to be felt and heard. This short passage from the introductory discourse indicates its style and method:

> Man is a rope stretched between beast and superman – a rope over an abyss.
> Perilous is the crossing, perilous the way, perilous the backward look, perilous all trembling and halting all the way.

> Man is great in that he is a bridge, and not a
> goal; man can be loved in that he is a transition and
> a perishing.
>
> I love him who lives that he may know, and who
> seeks knowledge that hereafter the superman may
> live; for thus he wills his own down-going.

Down-going translates "Untergang" inadequately. The German word means fall, collapse, decline, setting of the sun. Nietzsche means descent from what is now. It relates to the perishing of the old, also a new beginning.

> In the next discourse, the three metamorphoses
> of man are described.
>
> I declare the three metamorphoses of the spirit;
> how the spirit becomes a camel, the camel a lion, and
> the lion at length a child.
>
> The camel is the strong spirit able to bear the
> heavy burden in which reverence dwells.
>
> In the solitude of the desert, there comes the sec-
> ond metamorphosis: there the spirit becomes a lion
> that seeks to seize freedom as his prey and to contend
> for victory with the Great Dragon.
>
> But tell me, my brethren, what can the child do,
> which even the lion could not?
>
> The child is innocence and oblivion, a new be-
> ginning, a play, a self-rolling wheel, a primal motion,
> a holy yea-saying.

In our studies of philosophies, we are now in unknown territory. The language of the rationalists or the British empiricists is mostly acces-sible. The elements are familiar: mind, senses, transcendent, soul, physical. In the poetry and parables of Nietzsche, one can never be sure, as he states,

'I have always written my works with my whole body. I do not know what purely intellectual problems are."

The great problems all demand a great love, and of this only the strong, round, secure minds, resting firmly on themselves, are capable. It makes the most important difference, whether a thinker stands personally by his problems, so that in them he has his fate, his need, and also his best happiness, or whether he is 'Impersonal," i.e., only understanding how to grope for and hold them with the feelers of cold inquisitive thought. In the latter case, nothing will come of it.

In the Discourse called 'On Self-Surmounting," we read:

Wheresoever there is sacrifice and service, and appearance of love, there too is the will to be master. There creeps the weaker by secret ways into the citadel and into the very heart of the more powerful and there it steals power. And this secret life itself told me, 'I am that which must ever surmount itself."

In his book *Nietzsche and Christianity*, the philosopher Karl Jaspers has explored the many statements on Christianity and priests to be found in the complete works. 'We are no longer Christians. It is our piety itself, more severe and demanding, which forbids us today to be Christians." Elsewhere, we read: 'In spite of everything, Christianity is the best example of the ideal life that I have known; since I learned to walk, I have followed it and I believe in my heart, have never abused it."

Although most statements are antagonistic, there is no reason to suppose that the favorable ones are suspect. Such contradictions are many and are an essential part of the method.

Jaspers helps resolve the contradiction by distinguishing between the practice as Nietzsche saw it and what Christianity demanded. He compares the opposing attitudes of Nietzsche and Kierkegaard. The latter was firmly attached to his faith and remained bound to the Christian story "because his father told him it." Nietzsche was hostile to the story from the beginning. Kierkegaard was drawn into the depth of Christian theology; Nietzsche had no notion that theology had depths and had no interest in "these sublime edifices."

The damning criticism of morality as well as religion are prominent in commentators on Nietzsche, giving the impression that he despised them and his aim was to preach nihilism, the belief in nothing. In *Beyond Good and Evil*, this apophatic statement is written: "We want to be the inheritors of morality after we have destroyed morality." Surmounting can only be shown by way of contradiction.

Nietzsche refers many times to the will to power and the fact that leading National Socialists had the habit of sending *Thus Spake Zarathushtra* as a birthday present to comrades helped spread the notion that "power" means "political or military power." Nothing that Nietzsche wrote justifies this notion.

Nietzsche is always either showing the present or pointing to "what has to become." He does not declare the goal, what the future will be or a new age. The human being is "the becoming one" and only in the human being is the future. When he writes of the Eternal Return, he gives no indication of what that means. It is not just repetition. The journey of transformation doesn't stop. It always comes back to us. More he cannot say.

At the end of his book, Jaspers proposes two things one must bear in mind for a serious study of Nietzsche.

1. An idea, which suddenly comes to mind, is noted down on a piece of paper, and that becomes part of his "work." He may be just drifting around, far from his best thoughts, frivolous or even

fantasizing. His essential ideas, which belong to his fundamental understanding, are also noted down casually. One is not reading a finished work; on the contrary, one is in a workshop of thinking in which enduring results are created among innumerable crazy outbursts.

2. The work is overshadowed by the illness, which gradually affected him, and finally destroyed his sanity. In 1889 in Turin, Italy, a carter was beating his horse, which had fallen to the ground unable to rise. At the sight of this, Nietzsche stooped down and embraced the horse's head. At that moment, the darkness took over and lasted until his death in 1900. This illness does not discredit his work but asks for a truer understanding of the real message which he endeavored to leave us.

Rudolf Steiner (1861 — 1925)

Steiner was born to Austrian parents in a Slavic region of the Austro-Hungarian Empire, which is now Croatia. His father worked as a telegrapher in a station of the South Austrian Railway. The technology of the railway and the infant stage of the telegraph in a beautiful natural setting were part of Steiner's childhood. He was an unusually gifted child. At the end of his life, he wrote in his autobiography that he discovered geometry at the age of eight, which in his enthusiastic study confirmed for him that, as in geometry, it was possible to establish truths independent of any sense experience. This experience was especially significant as he was seeking a bridge between the intense clairvoyant perceptions, which accompanied him from childhood, and the normal world of the senses. He came to realize that sense-free experiences were also possible in our thinking.

At sixteen Steiner had already made an intensive study of Kant's *Critique of Pure Reason*, which is no easy task at any age. Instead of furthering studies in philosophy, he decided to enroll in the Technical University in Vienna, his principal subjects being mathematics, physics, biology, chemistry. He also studied philosophy with Franz Brentano and German Literature with Karl Julius Schröer. Both teachers made strong impressions on Steiner, and he lectured on the work of both in later years. The year after he left university, Steiner was asked to edit the Goethe-Schiller archives in Weimar. He spent seven years at this task. In the course of it he wrote *A Theory of Knowledge* in which he writes on themes that have come alive for him in his research on the work of Goethe and Schiller. The nature of experience, of perception and thought, of thinking as a higher form of experience and other philosophical themes are the content of the book. These provide an introduction to *The Philosophy of Freedom*, which he published eight years later. Steiner's essays on Goethe's scientific research were published as *Goethe the Scientist* after his death. In the chapter *Art and Science*, he discusses whether Goethe the poet and dramatist is a side of his personality distinct from the scientist or whether the two are bound together in such a way that the artist is unavoidably drawn to the very different discipline of science. The relationship of art to science is still a question today.

Since Descartes, at least, philosophers have felt obliged to describe their theory of knowledge or epistemology. They must explain how and why they understand the world and the human being in their way. Descartes begins with the thinking human being, Hume with one who gets sense impressions, and Spinoza with the idea of God. Yet we all look out on similar worlds, have similar needs, feelings, and other common features. What philosophers universally share is that the given world does not translate directly into the known world. Everything has its "why." So, philosophy is all about questions. Some may seem to have no answer. In stating their answers, philosophers then also seek to explain their methods or research processes. That is their theory of knowledge. This can be quite complicated. A particular theory can have far-reaching effects, not necessarily intended by the author. It may influence contemporaries and later generations in the way they look at life and how they act. While the cultural environment in which the theory is offered will invariably influence the reception it finds, this is not a judgment on the theory's coherence or depth. It may indeed be a response to a catastrophic experience such as a war or the plague.

Steiner wrote *Truth and Knowledge* for his doctorate in philosophy in 1892. In the first chapter he criticizes Kant's theory of knowledge, which is presented at the beginning of *The Critique of Pure Reason*.

Kant states the basic question, which he will deal with, as follows: How are synthetic judgments a priori possible? *The Critique of Pure Reason* will answer this.

The validity of his philosophy hangs on the answer to the question: Can one make valid statements which are independent of any experience?

Steiner investigates this question and finds that it is based on assumptions of which Kant seems quite unaware. He is writing more than a century after *The Critique* was written but the influence of Kant was still very much alive. Kant's theory had been criticized and condemned by other philosophers, but for other reasons. After analyzing the faults in Kant's theory in detail, Steiner lays the foundation for his own theory of knowledge. The work demands intensive study, which goes beyond the scope of this overview. However, two significant points need to be mentioned which Steiner considers a necessary basis for a theory of knowledge. Steiner states:

> The starting point of the theory of knowledge must lie outside the act of cognition. But it must be sought immediately prior to cognition, so that the very next step one makes beyond it is the activity of cognition. The absolute starting point must be determined in such a way that it admits nothing already derived from cognition. Only a directly given world picture can offer such a starting point.

This means that the theory must not begin, as with Descartes, with a cognitive statement, 'I think, therefore I am." What does Steiner mean by a directly given world picture? It seems to be a sense, feeling, or general apprehension of what being in the world is like for the author. Not what he has already chosen to believe, materialist or transcendentalist, utilitarian or spiritualist, etc. Is this possible? you may ask. We shall return to the question later.

The second point is the requirement of philosophy to distinguish between (a) what is given from nature and the world as well as inner events such as dreams, memories, feelings and (b) what the individual contributes in thoughts and understandings. This distinction needs careful and thorough consideration and is essential in following the development of Steiner's philosophy.

Four years after writing his doctorate, Steiner published *The Philosophy of Freedom*. This is his major philosophical work and represents a certain culmination. He referred to it throughout his life and also continued to write and lecture on philosophical themes. In 1901, he began to speak of his spiritual experiences, later founding the Anthroposophical Society, which enabled him to make significant contributions in diverse fields. Although there is some recognition of the results of his teaching (in education, agriculture, architecture, etc.), his claim to spiritual knowledge attracts much skepticism and even outright hostility as it is maintained such claims cannot be verified.

The Philosophy of Freedom has also been translated with other titles, e.g., *The Philosophy of Spiritual Activity,* or *Intuitive Thinking as a Spiritual Path.* Translations, especially in philosophy and literature, can be tricky. "Freiheit" in German has an emphasis less obvious in "freedom." Freedom can refer to political freedom and freedom from other forms of oppression imposed outwardly. It can also refer to inner restraints, like indoctrination, psychological conditions, influence of alcohol or drugs, fixed attitudes, all at various levels of importance for the individual. What *The Philosophy of Freedom* is concerned with is freedom in the way we come to our truth and the way we respond to situations that we meet, that is, knowledge and ethics.

The philosophy of the twentieth century and the first quarter of the twenty-first is concerned with relating the world to a lived reality. Philosophers of previous centuries had different matters to contend with. Now serious philosophical reflections have become existential. The exception to this is to view philosophy as subordinate to the achievements of science. *The Philosophy of Freedom* throws light on the existential issues of the twentieth as well as the twenty-first century. The book deals with the question of freedom, which embraces both knowledge and ethics. It will not compel or persuade you to arrive at any conclusions by appealing to evidence that you yourself cannot verify.

Why is this so? The very act of verification belongs to the act of thinking. Not Steiner's thinking, yours, the reader's. We are therefore looking for a method, not an answer we can retrieve from the shelf for use when needed. *The Philosophy of Freedom* is divided into two parts: Theory and Practice. In the preface we are presented with two guiding questions:

1. Can we understand human nature in such a way
   that this understanding serves as a support for all
   we may meet in the way of experience or science?

This challenges the prevalent views that the human being has only an animal nature or is, basically, a mechanism. If neither of these, what?

2. Can we ascribe freedom to ourselves?

Is this a yes/no question? A political question? A moral question? Is the human being able to make his own responsible decisions? Steiner states his concept of freedom in the following way:

Freedom is just as much a child of thinking, of
thoughts conceived not under duress from any outer
source, but in spiritual perception, as it is the child of
genuine, devoted love for the object of one's action.

To properly grasp Steiner's ideas, we need to understand what is meant by "spiritual perception" and "love for one's action."

The book begins with Steiner examining a number of ideas concerning freedom expressed by contemporary and past thinkers. A number of these refute the very idea of freedom. For them it amounts to the question of choice, and there are always external factors which determine our choices. Others simply maintain that the laws of nature make no exception to human behavior, which must follow its dictates, hence, no freedom. The key insight for Steiner is that human beings are able not only to be aware of their actions but also of the causes by which they are guided. For example, my decision to help someone may be in part in order to have a certain benefit for myself. To acknowledge this is liberating, to suppress it is self-deception. The one opens the way to freedom, the other blocks it. The belief that the brain determines behavior is another example of compulsion, which excludes freedom.

Another argument is that we are motivated by something outside (a wish to be rich?) but our character decides whether we respond to the motive. Hence, we cannot be free. Steiner distinguishes between an action "I have permeated with my consciousness" before acting and one "I just do without any clear reason."

Steiner then asks if the question of freedom to act can be considered by itself or whether there are other questions that are linked to it. He states as follows:

> If there is a difference between a conscious motive and an unconscious drive, then an act done out of the first must be judged differently from one done out of blind impulse. We tend to separate the human being into two parts, the knower and the doer. We tear apart the human being who is a whole and fail to acknowledge the human being who acts out of knowledge. It is said that we are free when we act out of reason and not out of animal desires. That says nothing. The question is: Do reason, purposes, and decisions exercise control over human beings in the same way as animal desires? If a reasonable decision rises in me of itself, with the same necessity as hunger or thirst, then I can only obey its compulsion, and my freedom is an illusion.

Further arguments deal with the question of the human will, which can be a difficult concept to explore. We easily recognize the results of our will. We walk, we speak, we do things, we understand, etc., all products of our will. But what is this which lies behind all our acts? We seem to be largely unconscious of this source. The arguments center on how we carry out a decision once it is made. Am I forced to act because of the strength of the motive? Can I be forced to do something I don't want to do? If so, there is no freedom.

The real question for Steiner is not whether I can carry out a decision once it is made but "how" the decision has been made. Rational thinking distinguishes the human from the animal in spite of the efforts of biologists to narrow or eliminate the difference. If the human will can be shown to be caused, like all other natural events, then human acts cannot be free. Clearly not all actions are free, but what about the actions for which the reasons are known? This leads to the question of the origin and significance of thinking and human cognition. Our actions are obviously not only due to rational deliberation but also to feelings like love, pity, ambition, generosity, and kindness. These cannot be reduced to rational concepts. Nevertheless, the question regarding the nature of human action presupposes that of the origin of thinking.

This question is the subject of the second Chapter, which includes the following statements:

> As human beings we are not organized in a fully integrated, unified way. We always demand more than the world freely offers. Nature gives us needs and the satisfaction of some of these she leaves to our own activity. The gifts allotted to us are abundant but even more abundant is our desire. We seem born for dissatisfaction. The urge to know is only a special case of this dissatisfaction.
>
> We receive a new problem with each phenomenon that greets us. Every experience becomes a riddle.
>
> We look everywhere for what we call an explanation of the facts.
>
> This search for explanation over and above what is given us splits us in two. The universe appears to us in two opposites: World and I. The barrier between

them comes with being conscious, but doesn't inhibit the feeling that they belong together. We are inside the world, not outside it.

In the final analysis, the whole spiritual striving of humankind consists in bridging this opposition. This striving belongs to religion and art as well as science.

This last statement may evoke comments and reactions on different levels. An important one is the level of language. The modern conceptualization of "religion" and "art" is quite different from that of the late nineteenth century. "Spirit" in English has some vague meanings like the "spirit of Shakespeare" or "they worked in a common spirit." In religion, it mostly refers to the Holy Spirit or a divine existence. The German word "Geist," translated as "spirit," is neither vague nor otherworldly. Any attempt to follow Steiner's thought requires an understanding of what he means by it. "Geist" is sometimes translated as "mind." Both words have interesting and slightly different ranges of meaning. In Steiner's writing, "Geist" cannot be pinned down to a narrow concept. The context will decide as well as the unprejudiced attentiveness of the reader. In *The Philosophy of Freedom*, thinking is referred to as a form of "spiritual activity" that is within the reach of the human being. It is essential to approach this concept of thinking without prejudice in order to properly understand the challenge Steiner sets out in this book.

Steiner goes on to examine the meaning and use of the concepts "Dualism" and "Monism." Dualism refers to the separation which consciousness makes between the world and I.

It may be between spirit and matter, subject and object, or thinking and phenomenon. The dualist is unable to find a bridge. Monism refers exclusively to unity and seeks to deny or erase the opposite. Steiner comments that neither is satisfactory as neither does justice to the facts. In the dualism of spirit/matter, the "I" is reckoned as an aspect of spirit. How could spirit (I) know what is going on in matter if matter is altogether foreign to spirit? And how could spirit affect matter so that intentions translate into deeds? Monism has attempted three solutions: (1) it denies spirit and becomes materialism, or (2) it denies matter, seeking salvation through spiritualism, or (3) it claims that matter and spirit are inseparably united so that it should come as no surprise if these two forms of existence, which are, after all, never apart, appear together in human beings.

For me, materialism can never be satisfactory, as every attempt to explain it must begin with forming thoughts. Immediately there are two worlds, the material world and the thoughts about it. Materialists ascribe the capacity to think to matter rather than to themselves. Then how does matter manage to think about its own existence? Some would claim that neuroscience brings evidence for the materialist, but there are also contrary views. One can also note that a mind has to interpret the evidence and if this mind is predisposed to a materialistic interpretation, then it will surely find one.

Goethe claimed that humanity has estranged itself from nature and must win its way back. To this, Steiner comments that we can only find nature outside us if we first know her within us. "What is akin to nature within us will be our guide. We do not want to speculate about the interaction of nature and spirit (mind). We have to descend into our own being to find there those elements we have saved in our flight from nature."

The investigation of our being must bring us the solution to this "riddle." Addressing the reader, Steiner continues:

> I am aware that some who have read to this point will not find my explanations correspond to "the present state of science." I can only reply that I have been concerned not with scientific results but rather with a simple description of what we all experience in our own consciousness. Everyday consciousness is unfamiliar with the sharp distinctions of science and

up to this, my intention has been to survey the facts of everyday life. What concerns me is how consciousness experiences itself hour by hour.

Steiner's methodology concerns the role of thinking in understanding the world. He introduces us to the crucial distinction between "percept" and "concept" in the following example of a game of billiards.

What happens when a billiard ball strikes another? The speed and movement of the second ball result from the impact of the first, uninfluenced by the player. He observes and forms concepts on different features of the event. What he sees or perceives are percepts. Concepts originate with the player (angle of impact, material of balls, surface, etc.). One may not think there is any difference between concept and percept, because as soon as one describes a percept, one is using concepts. When I look out of my window, I see shapes, colors, movement, change.

It is clear to me that all this is given. It is not me. If I want to describe the scene, I speak of trees, houses, sky, cars, etc., all concepts. This is my description. Another person's will be different. I do not produce what I perceive. Concepts, however, are not given; the observer supplies them. Why are we compelled to make concepts and where do they come from? An object or event without a concept is substantially changed when I find the concept, that is when I can identify it or explain it. Our percepts cannot as such be in error although our judgments as concepts can easily be wrong. The opposite view that our senses can be in error fails to distinguish between the judgment we make and the concept we apply to the percept. Hence, the example that mountains at a distance appear blue yet we know they are brown or green is not an error of the sense perception since we understand that the intervening atmosphere affects the color and is a part of the object.

Concepts are learned from other people and from books mainly in their usage. Observing a new object or event prompts us to find the appropriate concept. We may later re-evaluate these and change the concepts for ones better suited. This is the role of thinking. Observing and thinking are the two take-off points in understanding the world. They are the basis of everyday understanding as well as of complicated scientific investigations. A philosopher who wants to express first principles has to do so in concepts. Thinking must always be prior to any consideration of consciousness, feelings, willed activity.

Seeing a horse and thinking about a horse are two things that have separate sources in us. Observation comes before thinking. We often become aware of our thinking when we observe events both external and internal. There we become aware of a range of sensations, perceptions, feelings, memories, as well as concepts, etc. The next step is, for Steiner, the crucial one – observing my thinking.

I can also observe my thinking, but I cannot observe my thinking about an object when I am actually thinking. Ordinary observation is ongoing but observing my thinking is an exceptional activity. Thinking about thinking is not normal but it is normal about everything else. Observing feelings is not the same as observing concepts. A feeling of pleasure comes to me like tiredness or expectation. Thinking about a process has nothing to do with its effect on me. Thinking is an activity directed only to the object not to the thinker.

Our first observation about thinking is that it is the unobserved element in our mental activity. When I think, I do not look at my thinking, which I produce, but at the object, which I do not produce. Since we can know our thinking by observing past acts of thinking, we are able to know it more immediately and intimately than any other process. We can know where connections and relationships exist which are not so immediate in other processes. Observation of thunder and lightning does not give us the link. We can follow a train of thought without doing research. The transparency of thinking is completely independent of any knowledge of brain science.

Observation tells me that nothing guides me in combining my thoughts except the content of my thoughts. Observation of thinking is the most important observation that can be made. We look at our activity. We know how it comes about. We see through the connections. Now we are ready to turn to other observations.

> Thinking seems to dry out the life of the soul.
> Yet this is only the sharply contoured shadow of the
> reality of thinking – a reality interwoven with light,
> immersing itself with warmth in the phenomena of
> the world. This immersion occurs with a force that
> emerges in the activity of thinking itself – the force
> of spiritual love.

In the process that Steiner describes, the individual is discovering his own thinking. To accept current views that it is not adequate for the job or that its truth is dependent entirely on external evidence or mathematical logic is to resign the human being to a place with no exit.

The threat to human freedom today comes from several directions, from technology, from financial centers of power, from pandemics, from social instability, etc. Steiner writes: "Humans are free to the extent that they are able to obey themselves at each instance of their lives." Freedom is not a permanent achievement. Each new situation poses the question. One can only obey oneself if one knows oneself.

> To live in love of one's action and to let live in
> the understanding of the other's will, is the funda-
> mental maxim of free human beings.

> Our life is made up of free and unfree actions.
> Yet we cannot think the concept of what it is to be
> human without arriving at the free spirit as the pur-
> est expression of human nature. Indeed, we are only
> truly human to the extent that we are free.

Thinking gives us the capacity to understand the world. Our feelings are responses to our experiences in the world. Our actions are our effects on the world. Steiner examines in great detail the interplay of these forces, in our moral acts and in the purposes we give ourselves.

Only what a human being has made purposeful is purposeful as purposefulness arises only through the realization of an idea.

Human life has only the purpose and direction that a human being gives it.

What kind of task do human beings have? The one they set themselves.

In the contemporary world, Steiner's picture may seem to go beyond human possibility. If understood as a way rather than a goal, it rescues the human image from that of the mere animal and the insinuating machine.

Steiner's legacy embraces diverse fields of human endeavor. It not only includes his spiritual teaching but also practical applications in education, the foundation of schools incorporating methods to support the developing needs of children in opposition to the widespread "scientific" methods, the application of new methods in agriculture, the creation of new methods in medicine and therapeutic techniques. He was a sculptor, painter, and architect; he wrote and lectured extensively on social and economic issues. All this in the years following the I World War.

These initiatives should not be construed as final aims but to encourage fresh practice and thinking. For some, his spiritual teaching is the stumbling block. This should not be surprising considering the trend in recent times to conceive of the universe and the human being within the limitations of a broadly materialistic science. It would be naive to see this current paradigm as having the last word. The future it foreshadows is the mechanization of humanity. Steiner offers us another outlook.

With all the philosophers of the twentieth century, we can ask today about the relevance of their thoughts to the cataclysmic world we inhabit in the twenty-first century. There is an urgent need to understand it and to act. One thing seems clear. The way forward requires an awakening, a new vision, and the engagement of radical thinking. Thinking will need to be understood in its self-sustaining nature.

The concerns of philosophy in the twenty-first century will be centered on the issues of meaning and purpose in a world more and more shaped by technology and in which humanity has to confront itself on questions of race, gender, poverty/wealth, and most importantly, of what it means to be human.

This is a radically new situation. It has never been like this in the past. In Plato's time, there were skeptics who saw humans as playthings of the gods and life was about finding an antidote like hedonism or stoicism. In the thousand years after the Crucifixion, the hereditary gods began to lose their meaning. The birth of Christianity in Palestine was to provide a new meaning and a new religious practice in Western Europe. From the fifteenth century, the physical universe expanded for Europeans who now intensified exploration of the world, the investigation of nature, and understanding the role of the individual in society.

In philosophy, Descartes concentrated on the nature of mind to find a basis for knowledge. Others like Locke considered that the world we see is a sufficient basis upon which to build a knowledge of it. Kant retreated from this naive conjecture and asserted that human knowledge is limited and things-in-themselves cannot be known. Hegel opened new perspectives by rejecting the dichotomy of world and thought and taught that the ego is not a lonely entity in an alien world but an evolving self at home in a universe of reason. Kierkegaard complained that Hegel ignored human experience in favor of a machine-like system. Nietzsche then presented his unique challenge to current theories.

Darwin's theory of evolution unsettled beliefs in religion, history, and the nature of the human species. *The Origin of Species* was published in 1859. At the beginning of the century, Freud and Jung researched the human unconscious to cure the soul of its illnesses and discover its potential.

Edmund Husserl (1859 — 1938)

Our next philosopher, Edmund Husserl, developed phenomenology as a method for exploring human consciousness. In his words, "he wanted to found a new science, covering a new field of experience which had been in preparation since Descartes." Our main theme will be Phenomenology, but his studies and publications cover an extremely wide range.

He was born in Moravia, the son of non-orthodox Jews. His studies included mathematics, astronomy, physics, and philosophy. Later he continued his philosophy studies in Vienna under Franz Brentano whose lectures on psychology made a lasting impression on him. Husserl published *Ideas, General Introduction to Pure Phenomenology* in two volumes in 1913. He continued to refine his method into what he called "transcendental phenomenology." We take for granted in a naive way the nature of objects as we encounter them in everyday life and in ordinary science. Husserl's question was: What are the essential structures which allow objects to constitute themselves in consciousness? In other words, what role does the self play in knowing the world? He then opens up the realm of "Intentional consciousness." This will enable the phenomenologist to develop a radically new understanding of his/her basic views on the world and oneself and their rational interconnections.

An article by American Ronald H. Brady (former Professor of Philosophy at Ramapo College) entitled *Perception: Connections between Art and Science* will help us to understand what Husserl meant by "Intentionality." He describes a process of which we are not generally conscious, that in observing an object the mind is active in the act of observation. We don't see like a camera. We recognize.

Brady distinguishes between analytic knowledge and recognition. For example, a plant is classified by listing its characteristics, leaf shape, number of petals and stamens, color, fruit, etc. This is the method of classification and adds up to knowledge of the plant. In practice, the gardener mostly relies on recognition, which does not depend on a list of characteristics, but on other indicators like gesture, what it reminds you of, looks like a cat, or makes me feel happy. Not really characteristics, more like poetic similes. Not only gardeners, but also farmers, doctors, nurses, teachers use recognition and not analysis in daily practice.

The illustration will help us to experience what happens when we recognize an animal, for example. We don't summarize parts, we integrate them. The following exercise can show us what underlies the recognition process. A viewer will see either a duck or a rabbit.

The ambiguity of the design will allow the viewer to see either one or the other but not both at the same time. To move from one to the other, one can picture looking left (duck) or right (rabbit). This is different from a double-take where you cannot choose to go back to the first (mistaken) image. I was on a small plane flying to Germany. I woke up from a short snooze and looking out of the window, I saw a small branch with buds and no leaves upright on the wing. I then dozed off and on waking realized that I was seeing the lines between the wing plates and the studs. I could not now see the first image again. That is "double-take" in which I make a mistake and then I correct it. The duck/rabbit view requires an activity on my part. The viewer can now examine how they make the change. Does one just shift the direction of the eye? Or, while looking at the duck one thinks rabbit? Whatever triggers the shift we have to look at the figure in a special way if we are to recognize it. Notice that when the shift happens, the beak becomes ears and feathers become fur or the reverse. That means that the nature of the parts is not fixed but is flexible to fit the whole.

The mental activity by which we perform these recognitions is termed "Intentionality" in phenomenology. The term is reserved for that manner of thinking that formulates perception rather than reacts to it. One does not manufacture the process, nor does one "intend" the image. We intend the form of understanding that can grasp the image. We are "actualizing" the possibilities already inherent in the given situation.

Now if a change of understanding is all that is needed to bring about a change in perception, then either duck or rabbit is already an expression of a form of understanding rather than a perception to be understood. It seems that as we focus our eyes, we also focus our mind.

We can often see that a specific intentional decision was necessary to obtain the figure we are looking at. The following figure is made up of three "cheese wheels" with bits missing and three bent lines in a specific relation against an even white background.

Yet to the viewer the round wheels are readily understood as complete as is the underlying triangle and the partial slices of the wheels are hidden by the white triangle lying over them. It is the intentional understanding by which we take in the configuration that gives us the resulting figure. If we see the white triangle, we must understand the other parts, black circles and line triangle to be complete. The understanding is already in place if the white triangle is to appear.

In normal perception, we do not notice the preparation, as it remains unconscious, because we focus only on the perceptual result. Brady calls this process "aesthetic recognition," which is distinct from "analytic judgment" and explores its relationship to poetry and painting.

From Brentano, Husserl learned that there are two kinds of basic relations to the world: a primary one and a mental one. What is the primary one? It is based on immediate awareness of resemblance, difference, equality, degree, etc. The mental one is based on mental intentional acts – imagining, judging, willing, emotional acts. These are given in "Inner perception" and are, therefore, directly evident. A color, a tone, or a shape are primary but seeing a colored shape or hearing a note are mental and are distinguished from the objects we see or hear. Knowing something is different from what we know. It is the act which counts. Acts of believing, doubting, hoping (not beliefs, doubts, hopes) are intentional acts directed at something. Brentano and Husserl meant, it seems, not the usual relation of subject/object; I am seeing the tree, but a kind of act-object in which tree and I are both aspects of the act. This was later called "a relation of consciousness."

It may be helpful to know what Husserl opposed in order to understand what he promoted. For example, he maintained the concept of abstract ideas held by pragmatists like Locke was untenable. Locke assumed that the idea of a triangle is formed from the ideas we have of concrete triangles we have seen. The abstract idea would include all basic features, which belong to triangles but not be like any one of them. He considered such ideas as mere fictions, which help us to communicate. Hume thought that it was a matter of language, which enables us to assemble similar things. Husserl maintained that universals are quite different things from individual things. Similarity is unable to explain universals or abstract ideas. The fundamental issue is the intentional distinction between appearance and what appears in appearance. Brady's example above illustrates this point.

Husserl distinguishes between the act of consciousness and the phenomena at which it is directed. In order to be able to focus on the act of consciousness, he eliminated all reference to the external world. He called this "bracketing" (epoché). Objects don't just exist out there independent of us. By our being intentionally directed towards them we, in part, constitute them.

The word "phenomenology" has a very different meaning for Husserl from that of Hegel, whose *Phenomenology of Spirit* describes the progress of Spirit in a process of involution into history and human consciousness. Husserl is not concerned with such metaphysics. He examined, for example, the nature of meaning, which becomes part of phenomenological research. We observe the events and features in the world and in ourselves. Mostly we find them meaningful. Husserl's task was to study how meaning comes about.

We are surrounded by meanings. We live meanings. We know the meaning of a zebra crossing, traffic lights, and a large number of other signs on roads, in shops, in books, iPhones, and other things we use. These are many things we don't think of as having meaning because we are so used to them. Someone who has never seen a tap (faucet) does not know its meaning. When I lived in Paris in the 1950s, "Tabac" meant where I could buy stamps (as well as tobacco). So, doors, door-bells, and door-man all have their meanings. These are all signs. Expressions also have meanings. She smiled at me. He looked sad. I can't stand crowds. My daughter has just gone out (she goes for a walk). Blushing = embarrassed. Meanings are not necessarily correct. How do we construct them? Are they just habits?

What is the process that makes something meaningful or meaningless? In wakeful consciousness an endless sequence of images makes its appearances in the mind. Some are called up by the objects "out there," others by memory, imagination, feelings, and fantasy. Consciousness is not an empty space like a box open to be occupied. It is inseparable from it being "directed." It has "Intentionality." This does not imply that it is always intending something. It is not a psychological phenomenon like a complex or an archetype. It is an unconscious presence enabling one to grasp the world. Husserl's methods were designed to overcome what he saw as false theories and damaging presumptions in contemporary culture.

In a dualistic view of reality, two opposing principles exist which cannot be resolved into one. There is a modern assumption that religion is dualistic as it holds that there is a spiritual world and a physical world, two irreconcilable realities. Materialism claims to be monistic, as only one reality exists. The materialist believes that his view supported by the positivistic natural sciences is monistic. Phenomenology, which challenged this, must, therefore, be dualistic. Husserl undertook to repudiate this.

Descartes divided the world into two distinct entities, a thinking ego and an extended universe (res cogitans/res extensa). Husserl pointed out that science assumes that the extended world is grasped by means of mathematics, which measures, counts, and weighs. Intangible minds are situated in tangible living bodies, which allow the mind-part to be subjected to causality, measurement, and control. After exposing this reduction of the mind to mechanistic structures, Husserl then offers an alternative account of consciousness, which is both rigorous and related to lived experience. This brings him to a concept of embodiment. Husserl maintained that the tradition in dealing with psychophysical investigations, was to tie the "mind" to a material "body," assuming that this body is no different from any other spatial things. Although organisms belong to living things, they are nevertheless treated as subject to the same terms as inanimate objects and explained in terms of causal laws. Such assumptions ignore entirely what is essential to a body as a lived body experienced in a unique way by the embodied person. The attitude of the common approach ignores that the embodiment is not just a physical fact but is experienced directly from within. Phenomenology develops the theme of embodiment in great detail. In what is called the life-world (Lebenswelt), personal encounters are embodied encounters and our ongoing, everyday life is already an embodied one. The living body is the anchor for experience. It is not only the "here" from which perceptions and actions unfold, not an empty center but a filled one, with its own familiar feel, for to be embodied is to experience certain kinds of sensation as "mine" in a unique way.

Translating Husserl's language into common speech can give rise to two distinct ideas. In the descriptions of embodiment, he is saying what one seems to know already. On the other hand, the task he has taken on was to expose how one pictures what it is to exist, to be in this world, at levels both conscious and unconscious, in the first decades of the twentieth century. There is this body as a kind of object, ready to do what the mind or brain orders. To overcome this blind assumption, it is necessary to enter in imagination the reality of being embodied. In nineteenth-century novels, characters are given to expressing thoughts and feelings, which enable the reader to get inside the story. Virginia Wolfe presents life more through gesture, bodily conditions, thoughts that spring up in the encounters between characters and other such idiosyncrasies that allow us to glimpse hidden lives. Conscious intentions and aims are secondary. In 1916, Husserl was appointed full professor at Freiberg University and remained there until he was obliged to leave when the National Socialists came to power and decreed their race laws forbidding Jews to teach. He continued to write and lecture outside Germany until his death in 1937.

Martin Heidegger (1889 — 1976)

In one of the last lectures after the war, Heidegger addressed the question of thinking.

> We come to know what it means to think when we ourselves try to think. If the attempt is to be successful, we must be ready to learn thinking. As soon as we get involved in the attempt, we have to admit we are not yet capable of thinking. Yet man is called the being who can think. What is learning? We learn when we manage what we do so that it answers whatever essentials are addressed to us at any given moment. So learning to think is giving our mind to whatever there is to think about.
>
> Everything thought provoking gives us to think.
>
> Most thought provoking is that we are still not thinking. Even preoccupation with philosophy more than anything else may give us the stubborn illusion that we are thinking just because we are "philosophizing." We have still not come face to face with what intrinsically desires to be thought about. That we are not thinking, stems from the thing itself that must be thought about, that turns away from us, has turned away a long time ago.

Heidegger quotes this poem by Hölderlin:

> We are a sign that is not read.
> We feel no pain, we almost have
> Lost our tongue in foreign lands.

To understand what Heidegger meant by thinking, we face our first difficulty in his writings. These are hard to understand. Heidegger developed a personal vocabulary, which has to be learned, and especially when translated into English can be difficult to grasp hold of. Reviewers and commentators are obliged to spend time with the meaning of his language and sift it carefully before engaging in evaluating the content. This is not unusual in philosophy, but it is a considerable challenge with Heidegger.

Heidegger was born in Messkirch near Lake Constance of well-to-do parents of peasant stock. As a young boy, he spoke of "wanting to open up the vastness of the sky and at the same time to be rooted in the darkness of the earth."

In 1870, the split in the Catholic Church over the dogma of Papal Infallibility reached Messkirch. Roman Catholics were opposed to Old Catholics. The family supported the Romans and the official dogma. Heidegger served at mass and his education was supported by the church. At twenty, he began studying for the priesthood at Freiburg. Two years later, he abandoned theology and studied mathematics and philosophy. Drafted into a battalion in 1914, he was soon released for health reasons. In 1916, he met Husserl who had him appointed as a teacher. He married in 1917 and later his wife built his famous hut in Todtnauberg, where most of his cogitation took place. In 1919, he broke "with the dogmatic system of Catholicism." Through his teaching, he became known as an up-and-coming philosopher. In 1924, he had an intimate relationship with his gifted Jewish pupil, Hannah Arendt, who, after the Second World War, went on to write *The Origins of Totalitarianism.*

There seem to be three thinkers who strongly influenced the themes and the manner of discourse in philosophical circles in Germany and France in the first half of the twentieth century. Heidegger and Husserl discovered Kierkegaard and the task to investigate the nature of human subjectivity. Existentialism is applied to the different approaches to the question. The writings of Nietzsche gave permission to philosophers to ask new questions and reinterpret traditional themes. The third influence was Franz Brentano, the mentor of Husserl. The concept of "Intentionality," which was presented in Husserl's philosophy, originated with Brentano. That Heidegger was influenced by the work of the same thinkers as Steiner may seem surprising, but thoughts are not the exclusive possession of any author and can find their way to stimulate quite different worldviews.

In 1927, Heidegger published his major work, *Being and Time*. This placed him at the forefront of continental philosophers. *Being and Time* has been a major influence in European philosophy in the twentieth century. Its message might be opposed but not ignored by other philosophers. The message is complex, enigmatic, and difficult to access. Heidegger's personal vocabulary obliges the reader to look at familiar notions in a challenging new way. The central question addressed in the book is, What is 'Is"? Meaning: What is existence or being? This may seem absurdly simple. Does it indicate a loss or an avoidance at the heart of modern culture?

According to Heidegger, modern culture has lost Being, and that loss leaves us in a world of 'things"; people, plants, stars, ants, and atoms. These things, entities, are named 'beings" (no capital B) and their reality is derived from Being. In the Bible, God created the heavens and earth. He created the world out of nothing. The nothing out of which everything came is the Being we have lost. Heidegger asserts he is not referring to God. All his thinking is oriented to addressing our immediate world and existence in this world.

The meaning of 'Dasein" (to be there) is crucial for understanding the work. A common German word becomes a basic concept that resonates throughout his writings. At first, I supposed it was a metaphor for the human being but the text expressly rejects that. 'Dasein" might indicate 'presence" or 'to be open" as one commentator has suggested. It seems to point to a consciousness which the human being has the possibility to take on. In Heidegger's philosophy, the everyday human is 'Das man" (man = one or they). Another essential concept is Care (Sorge) and this word also has its own meaning. 'Care is the structure of the being of Dasein," Heidegger writes. In normal use, care is a psychological term indicating an attitude or relation to a person or object. With Heidegger, it points to being with and part of who and what is around (I have gleaned these interpretations from helpful commentators).

According to Heidegger, "Dasein" is prior to the distinction between thinking and willing or theory and practice. "Dasein" is "caring about." Care or interest in the world must precede questions about it. Concepts and judgements can be thought of as instruments for coping with the world. Heidegger adds other instruments with which the human being is in the world. The instance, which he uses to illustrate this, is the carpenter hammering in nails to clad a roof. The carpenter is absorbed in the activity to the extent that carpenter, hammer, and nail are a transparent unity. This reality is totally different from that of the thinking observer who stands apart from the world. "Dasein" is linked with time and its essence is an unfolding process, not a static condition.

The less we just stare at the hammer-thing, and the more we seize hold of it and use it, the more primordial does our relationship to it become, and the more unveiledly is it encountered as that which it is – as equipment. The hammering itself uncovers the specific "manipulability" of the hammer. The kind of being which equipment possesses – in which it manifests itself in its own right – we call "readiness-to-hand."

Heidegger stresses that his worldview is "In the world." There is no escape to a transcendent reality. "As Dasein, I ineluctably find myself in a world that matters to me in some way or another."

This is what Heidegger calls "thrownness" (Geworfenheit), a having-been-thrown into the world. I understand this to express that we don't arrive on Earth with "meaningfulness" as an attribute. It is not given. We have to acquire it, or rather, it is an aspect of "Dasein." My life is not circumscribed by what I now am and have been, and my potentialities are as essential to my being as my achievements. In defining what I am, the future has priority over the past and the present. All that one will do must terminate in death. Death intervenes between what I do and what I might do. Out of this arises guilt and anxiety.

Heidegger analyses the breakdown of ready-to, hand equipment and the subsequent revelation of the "world" through the phenomenon of "the unready-to-hand." When a tool breaks down or ceases to work properly, it quickly draws the attention of the user to the system of relations of which it is a part as it is directed toward a specific task. At the instant of breakdown, "Dasein" catches sight of everything connected to the work: the totality of the workshop, so to speak, is lit up. Anxiety induces a similar phenomenon, albeit on a larger scale, for in the moment of Anxiety's attunement, the entirety of "Dasein's" existence is disrupted. Its life no longer works, or functions with meaning. The argument, interwoven with similes and similarities, continues as follows:

At the moment anxiety swells, "Dasein" no longer feels at home within the comfort and safety of its inauthentic Being-in-the-world, as the thoughts and interpretations of the they-self (non- "Dasein") lose meaning. "Dasein" is forced before the "nothingness of existence." This primordial, "uncanny" existential mode of the "not-at-home" represents for Heidegger the most fundamental way of existence. Heidegger seems to say that when the individual is estranged, homeless, anxious, and has abandoned all the supports of the "everyday" existence, then it reveals the unique individual possibilities, which alone have the potential to enact as "Being-in-the-world." The reader has to accept that the notion of "Dasein" is real. Its existence, however, is asserted rather than demonstrated. The former thought structures in philosophy have collapsed. In these, thinking needed a priori judgements to be substantiated. Those judgments of the Heideggerian world stand by themselves and are substantiated by a process of interrelatedness and thoughtfulness rather than thinking.

Terms like "anxiety," "guilt," "resentment" and "homelessness" resonate powerfully in the twentieth-century consciousness. Related to "Dasein," they are changed to something else but the resonance remains. Does this association lend *Being and Time* a mood that accords with the despair and alienation of the time? Does it offer the individual a way of transformation, a step towards transformation?

"Authentic" is another important concept in Heidegger's vocabulary. The choices one makes are either authentic or inauthentic. It must be your choice and you must hold to it (resolve) in order to be authentic. The Greek word from which "authentic" is derived has a morbid association with killing and suicide. To be authentic is to kill off alternative inauthentic choices.

The question of freedom is considered at length in Heidegger's writings. Heidegger is clear about what it is not. His description of freedom opens up very important questions. He links indissolubly freedom and truth. Heidegger rejects what he considered the accepted truth, which is not just a recent misconception but goes back to Plato. Heidegger has at his service an enormous erudition that covers philosophy, mysticism, religion, history and the development of science. To challenge aspects of his worldview, one certainly needs resolve and authenticity.

Heidegger challenges the "rational animal" view of the human.

> Does the definition of man as the rational animal exhaust the essence of man?... Or does not the essence of man remain, does not the essence of being remain, and more dazzling, remain what is worthy of thought? Should we abandon this in favor of the madness of exclusively calculative thinking and its immense success?

There is a danger, writes Heidegger:

> Then there might go hand in hand with the greatest ingenuity in calculative planning and inventing indifference toward meditative thinking, total thoughtlessness. And then? Then man would have thrown away his own special nature – that he is a

meditative being. Therefore, the issue is the saving
of man's essential nature. Therefore, the issue is the
keeping meditative thinking alive.

He mentions "meditative thinking" and "meditative being" only vaguely as a possibility. Also, the reluctance to "meditative thinking" may be due less to thoughtlessness but more to do with a conscious opposition to the nature of spirit.

In *Being and Time*, Heidegger considers the significance of the Greek concept ἀλήθεια (*aletheia*) in order to understand the development of Greek thought as well as understand what he means by Being. The translation of Heidegger's use of the term (Unverborgenheit) is "unconcealment" or "disclosure." This is an important concept in Heidegger's understanding of truth. It stands opposed to truth expressed in propositional statements. He maintained that the translation usually used for "aletheia" (truth) is a later translation, and was not what Plato understood and implies the Greeks did not fully understand "aletheia."

Another interpretation gives a very different picture. Lethe means forgetfulness or oblivion. The prefix "a" is the negative. Hence, the Greek "aletheia" can be translated "unforgetfulness." Lethe is the river in the underworld, which the soul must cross on returning from previous existence. Having crossed Lethe, the soul forgets its pre-life experience. However, it can recover a lost knowledge in this life. This is demonstrated in Plato's dialogue, *Meno*, in which Socrates questions a slave concerning a geometrical figure to prove that knowledge is a remembering. Steiner in his lectures on Greek thought opens up the meaning of "aletheia" to give a very different interpretation from Heidegger.

In the essay, *On the Essence of Truth*, written in 1943, Heidegger describes the relationship of freedom to truth. Freedom is "letting be." He does not mean it in a negative sense.

To let be is to engage oneself with beings. On the
other hand, to be sure, this is not to be understood

only as the mere management, preservation, tending, and planning of the beings in each case encountered or sought out. To let be – that is, to let beings be as the beings which they are – means to engage oneself with the open region and its openness into which every being comes to stand, bringing that openness, as it were, along with itself. Western thinking in its beginning conceived this open region as 'ta aletheia," 'the unconcealed."

Does he mean letting happen what is able to emerge without 'Interference" from the meddling intellect? This could imply a true awareness is what is needed and the notion 'unconcealment" would favor this. Here I am prompted to raise the question concerning the role of the 'I" within that process.

Shortly after Adolf Hitler came to power on January 30, 1933, Martin Heidegger was installed as Rector of Freiberg University on the recommendation of his predecessor von Möllendorff, who was forced to resign after he had refused to display an anti-Jewish poster. Ten days later, Heidegger became a member of the Nazi party. And remained a member until the party was dissolved in 1945. How a member of a political movement that brought about the Holocaust can teach about the nature of freedom is a question that has confounded and disturbed many readers of *Being and Time.*

In November 1933, Heidegger addressed the six hundred students of Freiberg University with the following words:

The Nationalist Socialist revolution is bringing about the total transformation of our German existence (Dasein). In these events, it is up to you to remain the ones, who always urge on and are always ready, the ones who never yield and who always grow....You are obligated to know and act together in the creation of the future university of the German spirit. Let your loyalty and will to follow be daily and hourly strengthened. Let your courage grow without ceasing so that you will be able to make the sacrifices necessary to save the essence of our Volk, and to elevate the innermost strength of the state. Heil Hitler.

Heidegger's early membership of the Nazi Party and support at the time for the Hitler project, the nature of which was clearly visible, makes him a highly controversial figure. Heidegger resigned the rectorship the following year and claimed that thereafter he pursued an independent course. When his mentor, Husserl, was forced to resign from the chair of Philosophy at Freiberg because of his Jewish background in 1936, Heidegger replaced him.

Even after the war, Heidegger never made any gesture to reassure his admirers or to answer his critics concerning his relationship to the ideology of Nazism. Whether he ever changed his views remains unclear and as a result, he has been widely condemned. However, he also had his supporters who were prepared to set aside his former role in the Nazi party and recognize his philosophical contribution on its own terms.

This raises the question about the relationship between a philosophy and the personality of the philosopher. In Heidegger's case, it appears that he identified so closely with his philosophy that the teaching was inseparable from the teacher. Can his contribution be freed from his practice and worldview? Is philosophy, the love of wisdom, really possible under such conditions? I leave this as an open question for the reader.

Bertrand Russell (1872 — 1970)

Russell was a member of the British aristocracy as an Earl and a Viscount. His grandfather was Lord John Russell, the liberal Prime Minister who enabled the passing of the Reform Act in 1832, which was a major step in extending the voting rights. Bertrand Russell's godfather was the philosopher John Stuart Mill. He therefore came into the world not only with a silver spoon in his mouth, but nurtured in the liberal ideals of his grandfather and the impulses for social over private and individual well-being of his godfather. In his *Autobiography*, he assesses his life as follows:

> Three passions, simple but overwhelmingly strong, have governed my life: the longing for love, the search for knowledge, and unbearable pity for the suffering of mankind. These passions, like great winds, have blown me hither and thither, in a wayward course, over a great ocean of anguish, reaching to the very verge of despair.
>
> I have sought love, first, because it brings ecstasy – ecstasy so great that I would often have sacrificed all the rest of life for a few hours of this joy. I have sought it, next, because it relieves loneliness – that terrible loneliness in which one shivering consciousness looks over the rim of the world into the cold unfathomable lifeless abyss. I have sought it finally, because in the union of love I have seen, in a mystic miniature, the prefiguring vision of the heaven that saints and poets have imagined. This is what I sought, and though it might seem too good for human life, this is what – at last – I have found.
>
> With equal passion I have sought knowledge. I have wished to understand the hearts of men. I have wished to know why the stars shine. And I have tried

to apprehend the Pythagorean power by which number holds sway above the flux. A little of this, but not much, I have achieved. Love and knowledge, so far as they were possible, led upward toward the heavens. But always pity brought me back to earth. Echoes of cries of pain reverberate in my heart. Children in famine, victims tortured by oppressors, helpless old people, a hated burden to their sons, and the whole world of loneliness, poverty, and pain make a mockery of what human life should be. I long to alleviate this evil, but I cannot, and I too suffer. This has been my life. I have found it worth living, and would gladly live it again if the chance were offered me.

Throughout much of his life, Russell saw himself primarily as a writer rather than as a philosopher. Our main interest is the philosopher hoping for depth of understanding and where there is also breadth of experience, we value that too.

When he was still a child, both parents died and a few years later his grandfather also, which resulted in his grandmother taking charge of his upbringing. She was particularly concerned to ward off the atheists who threatened to influence him.

When he was eighteen, Russell began his studies in mathematics and morals at Trinity College, Cambridge. A year after graduating, he married for the first of four times. While he was still in his twenties, he began work on logic with the philosopher A. N. Whitehead. This work occupied them over ten years and resulted in the three volumes of *Principia Mathematica*.

Logic is not a big draw for most people in spite of its importance. Aristotle initiated the study of logic as a tool that underlies all kinds of knowledge and a necessary step for learning. It enables one to identify if an argument is valid or invalid. This tool continued to serve unquestioned until the nineteenth century when George Boole and Gottlob Frege extended the scope of logic to address new questions. Fundamental to these was whether mathematics is a branch of logic, and if all mathematical theorems can be recast as logical proofs. Russell and Whitehead set about to resolve these new issues. The *Principia Mathematica* is a high point in the achievement of Russell and Whitehead. Russell also used logic to clarify issues in philosophy. His Analytic Philosophy deals with the nature of knowledge, metaphysics, ethics, and politics.

According to Russell, it is the philosopher's job to discover a logically ideal language – a language capable of describing the world in such a way that we will not be misled by the accidental, imprecise surface structure of natural language. Russell writes in *The Scientific Outlook* as follows:

> Ordinary language is totally unsuited for expressing what physics really asserts, since the words of everyday life are not sufficiently abstract. Only mathematics and mathematical logic can say as little as the physicist means to say.

Russell explains, as follows, the train of thought which brought him to this view which is named Analytic Philosophy. This is described in *The Problems of Philosophy*, which he published in 1912.

> In daily life we assume as certain, many things which, on closer scrutiny, are found to be so full of apparent contradictions that only a great amount of thought enables us to know what it is that we really may believe. In the search for certainty, it is natural to begin with our present experiences, and in some sense, no doubt, knowledge is to be derived from them. But any statement as to what it is that our immediate experiences make us know is very likely to be wrong. It seems to me that I am now sitting in a chair,

at a table of a certain shape, on which I see sheets of paper with writing or print.

We recall Descartes sitting in front of a stove in Holland searching for something he could not doubt. A few centuries later Russell is sitting in a room in Trinity College, Cambridge. They seem to have similar questions but the answers will be very different. What has changed? Like Descartes, he is not quite sure that he is sitting somewhere. Russell questions everything out there. He is sure it is not telling him the truth. Descartes looks inward and finds his "cogito" or "mind" which promises the truth.

Russell continues his reflections by informing us what he sees as he turns his head and looks out the window. He also tells us what he believes, for example that the sun is a hot globe. He also believes that anyone coming into the room would see the same chairs, etc. This is all so evident, he writes, it is hardly worth stating except to someone who doubts that I know anything. And there are good grounds for doubting, he opines. Citations will be from the *Problems of Philosophy* unless noted otherwise.

To make our difficulties plain, let us concentrate our attention on the table. To the eye it is oblong, brown and shiny, to the touch it is smooth, cool and hard; when I tap it, it gives out a wooden sound. Anyone else who sees, feels and hears the table will agree with this description, so it might seem as if no difficulty would arise; but as soon as we try to be more precise our troubles begin. Although I believe the table is "really" of the same color all over, the parts that reflect the light look much lighter than the other parts, and some parts look white because of reflected light. I know that if I move the parts that reflect, the light will be different so that the apparent distribution of colors on the table will change. It follows that if several people are looking at the table at the same moment, no two will see exactly the same distribution of colors, because no two of them see it from the same point of view, and any change in the point of view makes changes in the way light is reflected.

For ordinary folk the above train of thought is obvious and trivial but the philosopher has stumbled on the problem of the distinction between "appearance" and "reality." For the philosopher, this problem arouses his desire to know and understand, facing up to all the difficulties which have little interest for the practical man.

Russell continues his argument. "To return to the table, it is evident from what we have found, there is no color which pre-eminently appears to be the color of the table." This seems to indicate that if there are two tables in the room, one light brown and the other ebony black, Russell would have difficulty in choosing if a friend opened the door and asked if he could borrow the light brown table. He has explained the special interest of the philosopher as opposed to that of the practical man. Nevertheless, it is important the philosopher stays within the world he is studying and not find equivalences which he has imported. The sun can be red, orange, yellow, and white. These changes are caused by phenomena external to the sun just as changes in the color of the table are caused by phenomena external to the table.

Russell's doubt is applied to other sensory data and confirms for him that the world given to us by eye, ear, touch, etc., cannot be relied on and we must look elsewhere for a sound basis for knowledge. He considered the philosophy of Berkeley who maintained that all experience was a property of the mind and we cannot know what is out there in the world of matter. Before dealing with the question of the existence of matter, Russell reminds us where we have got to.

It has appeared that if we take any common object of the sort that is supposed to be known by the senses, what the senses immediately tell us is not the truth about the object as it is apart from us, but only the truth about the sense data which as far as we can see depend upon the relations between us and the object. Thus, what we directly see and feel is merely "appearance" which we believe to be a sign of some "reality" behind and beyond. But if the reality is not what appears, do we have any means of knowing whether there is any reality at all? And if so, have we any means of finding out what it is like?

Now we read of the crucial, unavoidable issue on which, if possible, reality can find a base.

We have to ask ourselves whether, in any sense at all, there is such a thing as matter. Is there a table which has a certain intrinsic nature and continues to exist when I am not looking, or is the table merely a product of my imagination, a dream-table in a very prolonged dream? This question is of the greatest importance. For if we cannot be sure of the independent existence of objects, we cannot be sure of the independent existence of other people's bodies, and still less, other people's minds, since we have no grounds for believing in their minds except such as are derived from observing their bodies.

Thus, if we cannot be sure of the independent existence of objects, we shall be left alone on a desert island. Also, we shall be unable to be sure of the desert island!

This is an uncomfortable possibility; although it cannot be proved false, it is equally incapable of being proved true, Russel assures us. He now looks for a fixed point from which to start. Although he doubts the physical existence of the table, he does not doubt the existence of the sense-data which made him think there was a table. Then follows a brief description of Descartes' viewpoint. Russell remarks that the existence of the "I" is as difficult to prove as the existence of the table.

To prove the existence of matter we can rely on common sense, writes Russell. This seems rather unsatisfactory considering the low opinion he has already expressed on a common-sense view of sense-data. Sense-data means all that we perceive whether outside us like a table or inside us like a feeling. Sense-data includes feelings, memories and past thoughts, dreams, ideas, suggestions and plans and all that we perceive whether outer or inner.

To the question, "Is there something which persists other than sense data when I go out of the room?" Russell replies: "Common sense unhesitatingly answers that there is." It would be plainly absurd to suppose otherwise. If the cloth entirely hid the table and the table ceased to exist, the cloth would be miraculously suspended in mid-air, which would be absurd.

In the course of this argument, Russell admits that we can never prove the existence of things other than ourselves and our experiences. Yet he maintains that it is the likeliest solution. Russell hates dogmatism in any form.

The next line in his argument is to show by the example of color which we experience and yet know from experiment that its transmission is by colorless particles called photons. Appearance (color) and reality (photons) are now explicit. Science has given us the answer which philosophers like Kant looked for and failed to find. The belief that colors conveyed by colorless photons to the eye and hence by colorless nerves to the brain where they appear (although still seen "out there") turns out to be a circular argument. This is the basis for Russell's reality!

Elsewhere, Russel maintains that there is no fundamental distinction between matter and mind. This may contain a deep truth but it should not confuse us in observing the human activity in the search for truth.

In great music and art, we can discern truth, possibly. Is there a kinship between the search for truth and the search for meaning? It seems to me they cohabit. Error offends the search for meaning.

Our ability to think, a property of the mind is given to us. It's what makes us human, according to Aristotle. My thoughts, produced by my thinking, however, are not given. Once I have made them, I can look at them as objects. If Russell did not produce his thoughts, why put them in a book and sign it? When I read them, I experience myself thinking them although someone else has produced them.

For example, most of us have learned the theorem of Pythagoras. When one has understood it, one sees that the argument is valid. There is no need to measure lots of triangles to prove it. Thinking and thinking alone gives the proof. Notice, we have two kinds of given. Sense-data is given without any activity on my part. Thoughts applied to sense-data are given by the person thinking them. In the meeting of these two, sense-data and concepts, understanding arises. This gives confidence that the phenomenon is real. If the thinking is determined by some outside influence such as brain processes, it is no longer thinking and philosophy books are superfluous. Thinking produces concepts which enable us to know reality and to find meaning.

In the house next door to where my wife and I once lived, a little child ran inside and excitedly said to his mum, "Butterflies, butterflies!" Mum ran out and saw to her horror a swarm of bees. From this experience the child learned a new concept, bee. As we grow up, we accumulate concepts. Concepts give us the possibility to connect with other concepts which can help us to understand fresh sense-data. The concept "temperature" connects us with "fever," "climate," "bath," "cooking," and many more concepts. The richer our conceptual life the more possibilities we have for understanding and enjoyment.

Our sense experiences give us our individual world from our individual perspective. They do not isolate us from each other but make our humanity endlessly diverse and rich. In an avenue of trees, the near ones appear tall, the far ones short. From the other end the sense-data is reversed. So, sense-data can differ according to the position of the viewer and also according to physiology, being deaf, color-blind, or completely blind. I once had a green van which a color-blind friend saw as brown. That did not make me doubt the color of my van. The concept of color-blindness linked his sense-data with my understanding.

Russell is justified in stating that sense-data does not give a shared world which we can all agree on. For that we have to go beyond our individual experience and we can only do that by thinking and developing concepts. Russell writes that we can go beyond the limits of our private experience by the experience of the knowledge of description. What is this? Russell distinguishes two kinds of knowledge of things:

(a) Knowledge by acquaintance. Anything of which we are directly aware without the intermediary of any process of inference or any knowledge of truths. For Russell, it is a direct causal interaction between a person and some object that the person is perceiving.

(b) Knowledge by description refers to physical objects including living objects and also other people's minds.

Whereas knowledge by description is something like ordinary propositional knowledge, e.g., 'I know that snow is white," knowledge by acquaintance is familiarity with a person, place, or thing, typically obtained through perceptual experience, e.g., 'I know Sam," 'I know the city of Bogotá." Other examples, 'I know my dog" and 'I know my neighbor's dog" are known by acquaintance. President Putin's dog, the species 'dog" and the dogs which reached the South Pole with Amundsen we know by description. Every proposition like 'I know that London is in England" which we can understand must be composed wholly of constituents (city, country, etc.) with which we are acquainted. In other words, we can only say what we are already acquainted with our bare selves as opposed to our thoughts and feelings. He assures us: "Nevertheless, there are some reasons for thinking that we are acquainted with the I."

Knowledge of General Principles. This is in addition to knowledge of things. These are truths which we do not challenge. Arithmetic truths, $5 + 7 = 12$. Induction, the road is wet because it has rained. Logic and the laws of thought which refer to theories of mathematics and probabilities.

The idea or concept "knowledge" has different applications. I know French. I know how to make bread. I know your friend Charlie. I know how the lawn-mower works. I know my feelings. I would like to know your thoughts. All these somewhat different kinds of knowing present no difficulty to the common understanding. When the philosopher or scientist searches for knowledge, they have a process in mind, and essential to that process is thinking. We use "thinking" in a loose way when we are just expressing an opinion. Philosophers and scientists have another "thinking" in mind. It has to take place in somebody's mind, where it formulates concepts. Through concepts others will understand, or not, what that somebody thinks. If not, they use thinking to clarify. When issues arise such as "do parallel lines meet at infinity," only thinking can deal with them. Mountains seen at a distance appear blue. Thought connections resolve the apparent illusion. Does that make the senses untrustworthy? We may need further research which thinking will propose. If we cannot prove that the speed of light is constant in the universe, we make a hypothesis which thinking acknowledges.

Russell's two kinds of knowledge fail to give to thinking the prime role which it has in our mental life when we undertake to know the world and the self. Kant's observation that "percepts are blind without concepts and concepts are empty without percepts" seems appropriate.

The distinction between concept and percept is a major source of misunderstanding in some twentieth-century philosophy. Part of the difficulty is that when we perceive an object like a table, we have already united the concept "table" with the sense-data. So, we don't notice the role thinking plays. It can also have the consequence in modern life that we don't observe the sense-data. Our ability to observe our surroundings today is noticeably weak.

Objects can be conceived in different ways. For the Spanish conquerors of Peru, the Bible was a sacred object, for the Inca king a devilish object and perhaps today a door-stopper. The concepts we use can show our values and relationship to objects. "Soil" became "dirt" in the industrial cities of Britain. Not something essential for plant life but something to get rid of. "Lady" changed its meaning as the class system lost its hold. Today descriptive words are being lost in everyday language and with them observations.

In addition to Russel's two kinds of knowledge – knowledge by acquaintance and knowledge by description – he also, in "General Principles," points to the elements that belong to thinking itself, induction and deduction and the laws of thought e.g., syllogisms. Aristotle contributed "logic" or "the laws of thought" and later thinkers have confirmed them after thinking about them. *Principia Mathematica* had the aim of establishing a firm foundation for mathematics as an extension of logic. The elements it deals with, types, contradictions, etc., are all products of thinking. The genius of the Austrian philosopher and mathematician Kurt Gödel was to demonstrate unavoidable contradictions or limitations to the arguments (incompleteness) in *Principia Mathematica*. His method was thinking.

No thinking is final. New percepts like the other side of the moon feed into our conceptual life. Astronomy has to develop new concepts to deal with new data provided by technology. I think that Russell would be in agreement with most of my comments, even about the centrality of thinking. He confines philosophy to the methods of science which demand evidence for its claims. He gives priority to the physical world and avoids in his philosophy the unexplored inner life and its interrelationship with the outer. He reserves his healthy attitudes to the human dilemmas in his engagements with social, political, and educational issues. At the end of *The Problems of Philosophy*, Russell writes:

> The value of philosophy is to be sought largely in its very uncertainty. While diminishing our feeling of certainty as to what things are, it greatly increases our knowledge as to what they may be; it removes the somewhat arrogant dogmatism of those who have never traveled into the region of liberating doubt, and it keeps alive our sense of wonder by showing familiar things in an unfamiliar aspect.
>
> All acquisition of knowledge is an enlargement of the Self...

Such sentiments restored for me somewhat the value of *The Problems of Philosophy*. However, the last quote reads, 'but this enlargement is best attained when it is not directly sought." Unfortunately, he does not explain how that is done. It is a strange comment which has little to do with philosophy. For me, philosophy is best when it sheds light and faces contradiction and puzzlement. Nothing is to be dismissed for the sake of comfort. It has to embrace experience in depth as well as in breadth. It can include and go beyond the objective thinking of science without rejecting its independence from dogma and prejudice. It means the development of the inner activity of mind as well as its robust applications to human needs.

In 1946 Russel published *History of Western Philosophy*. It gives comprehensive accounts of Ancient Philosophy from the pre-Socratics to Plotinus, of Catholic Philosophy from the religious development of the Jews through the Church Fathers and the Schoolmen to Aquinas and finally, of Modern Philosophy from the Italian Renaissance to the last chapter on Logical Analysis. It is a scholarly work presenting from a modern perspective the vast range of European thought. I should add, 'from an

Anglo-Saxon modern perspective" as continental writers would have a different perspective. At the end of his history, he writes:

> In the welter of conflicting fanaticisms, one of the few unifying forces is scientific truthfulness, by which I mean the habit of basing one's beliefs upon observations and inferences as impersonal and as much divested of local and temperamental bias, as is possible for human beings. To have insisted upon the introduction of this virtue into philosophy, and to have a powerful method by which it can be rendered fruitful, are the chief methods of the philosophical school of which I am a member.

In the year the *History of Western Philosophy* was published, the first Macy conference was held in New York. It was attended by a remarkable group of scientists, mathematicians, and logicians and the purpose was to set the foundations for a general science of the workings of the human mind. There were huge hopes that at last one could construct a scientific theory of the mind and so solve the ancient problem of mind and matter. Then 'mind" would find its rightful place in nature.

Philosophy has become a technical problem. This dream is with us today with all its attendant dangers. The Analytic Philosophy of Russell seems to subscribe to this goal.

In addition to his work on mathematics, logic, and philosophy, Russell had wide interests which made him a popular lecturer. He was invited to address audiences on both sides of the Atlantic as well as in Europe. Ideas on education, votes for women and the aims of liberals were among his concerns. He founded a school based on his views and in politics canvassed three times unsuccessfully for election to Parliament. He was a committed pacifist and during World Wars I and II, he spoke publicly against war. During both he was fined and had to serve prison sentences. He was also a committed atheist and on two occasions invitations to lecture to students were withdrawn in order to protect a vulnerable audience from his dangerous opinions. His anti-religion views were directed more against practices in religions such as dogmatism and false presentations, than against religious feelings.

After the Second World War, he wrote and demonstrated publicly against the spread of nuclear weapons. In 1957 with Einstein, he founded the Pugwash Conferences on Science and World Affairs based in Canada. Its aim was to control and eliminate weapons of mass destruction. The conference still meets annually.

The story of Russell's life reflects in many ways the history of his century. The social changes, scientific developments, technological advances, extreme political doctrines, destructive wars on an unimaginable scale, he experienced them all at close quarters. People and human relations were important for him. Yet he seems to have two distinct sides to his personality. On the one hand, there is the side expressed in his philosophy. The scientific method is for him the one route to build knowledge of the world. He has no interest in the questions of the self which preoccupied continental philosophers like Husserl and Heidegger.

In his book *Man or Matter*, Ernst Lehrs (1894–1979) described modern man as "a one-eyed color-blind spectator." Typically, he is an observer perhaps sitting in a chair looking at a table, a spectator, separate and isolated from the world. He is color-blind as the world he seeks to know has no color. The color we believe is out there, is in fact produced in the brain. He is one eyed. The French philosopher, Bergson, compared the world of the mathematician to a "cinematograph." The movie camera reel consists of a sequence of images, a discontinuous stream of bits, which give the impression of wholeness. The movie camera is one-eyed. Russell with his many gifts, as philosopher, seems to typify "the modern man."

Integrity and honesty were deeply rooted in his character. He was a humanist in the tradition of the eighteenth century, a firm believer in liberal values, a fighter for freedom of thought with genuine sympathies for the victims of modern society. Although not given to too much intro-spection, he had good judgment in social and political matters. His wide interests and gift for friendship explain his popularity and the large appre-ciation for his writings and public lectures.

Ludwig Wittgenstein (1889 — 1951)

In autumn 1911, Ludwig Wittgenstein arrived at Trinity College, Cambridge to be a research student with Professor Bertrand Russell. The meeting was to have momentous consequences for both. Wittgenstein had been doing research in the design of aircraft engines at Manchester University for about two years and in the course of his work was drawn into mathematical studies. He read Russell's *Principia Mathematica* and was tempted to abandon aeronautics and pursue philosophy. He consulted with the mathematics professor Gottlob Frege who suggested he visit Russell. Russell accepted him as his student, not knowing his capabilities but quickly realizing he was meeting an unusual personality. Russell recalls that where other students took notes and asked questions as was normal, "the German," as Russell called him, engaged in discussion, argued and pressed his own viewpoints. He was passionate, enthusiastic, obsessive, intolerant, and irritating. In spite of his behavior, Russell came to see he was dealing with a genius and a warm and appreciative friendship grew between them. Russell began to think this student was the one capable of continuing his work. Meetings continued to be stormy and hurtful but also creative. Wittgenstein was full of praise for the *Principia Mathematica* but dismissed as trivial *The Problems of Philosophy*, which Russell was publishing.

Who was this "German"? He was Austrian, from Vienna, the eighth and youngest child of the steel manufacturer, Karl Wittgenstein, one of the richest men in the Austrian Empire. The family was Jewish and integrated into the rich cultural life of the capital. Vienna was the birthplace of atonal music, the stark functional style of modern architecture, the Jugendstil movement in art, and psychoanalysis. Later it was also the birthplace of Zionism and Nazism. Karl Kraus, journalist and satirist, named Vienna "the research-laboratory for world destruction."

At the age of eight, Ludwig paused in a doorway to reflect on the question, "Why should one tell the truth if it is to one's advantage to tell a lie?" He had a compulsion to face such questions. Philosophy came to him, not he to philosophy. Its dilemmas were experienced as unwelcome intrusions, which held him captive, and he was unable to get on with everyday life until he had solved them.

Of the eight children, Hans, the oldest brother, was a musical genius who committed suicide after escaping family pressure by traveling to America. Later a second brother, Rudolf, also killed himself. Paul, who lost his right arm in the Great War, became a successful concert pianist. Ravel's *Concert for the Left Hand* was written for him. As a child, Ludwig showed no special gift but a leaning to the practical. Yet a deep connection to music, art, and literature developed in him. He tolerated no music composed after Brahms. He said, "Even in Brahms I hear the sound of machinery. The true Sons of God were Mozart and Beethoven."

Wittgenstein went to the Realschule in Linz where Hitler had also been a pupil. At nineteen, he went to Manchester University to study aeronautics and became one of the leading authorities on the subject. His interest in philosophical and moral questions was temporarily suppressed until he read Russell's *Principles of Mathematics*, an earlier publication to the later *Principia Mathematica*, which was also published when Wittgenstein finally reached Cambridge. "My intellect never quite recovered from the strain," Russell confessed about the result of years of difficult and strenuous thinking. In those years at Manchester, Wittgenstein was several times on the verge of suicide. It was Russell's recognition of his abilities and his realization that philosophy was his home that rescued him. At twenty-four and still an undergraduate, he was already recognized as the equal of his master. In 1913, Wittgenstein decided he needed to get away from the scholarly circles at Cambridge and isolated himself in Norway for a period, confiding in Russel that he prostituted his mind talking to intelligent people. He then returned to Vienna and, as the war loomed, enlisted for military service. He was rejected on grounds of health, but determined to get involved, he volunteered for medical service. He was determined to confront challenges, even existential risks that did not require intellectual work. He expressed the desire to change into a different person. His reading at the time included Nietzsche, St Augustine, Kierkegaard, Tolstoy, and studies on Christianity.

While serving as an artillery soldier on the Russian front and later, on the Italian front, Wittgenstein continued to develop his philosophical ideas. When the war ended, he completed a draft of his work in a prisoner-of-war camp from which he was released in 1919.

The work was published in 1920, the only complete book published during his lifetime. Its eventual titl,e by which it is now known, is *Tractatus Logico-Philosophicus*. It immediately created a stir. Russell wondered what it was saying. It was debated in the Vienna Circle, a select group of philosophers with divergent viewpoints who invited Wittgenstein to Vienna to discuss his ideas. Wittgenstein turned up but spoke about poetry, refusing to talk about the content of his book. Since its appearance, the *Tractatus* has been understood in a variety of ways. For some, it underpins the view that the scientific method is basic to philosophy (akin to Russell's view), for others it is almost a mystical text. Sections of the book are acceptable to some philosophers who strongly oppose other sections. Wittgenstein was of the opinion that he had now resolved the main problems of philosophy and so decided to abandon it.

The *Tractatus* explores the philosophical problems of the limits of the world, of thought and of language, and of what can be meaningfully said about them. However, there is a whole world that can only be shown. It asserts that much of philosophical debate has been pointless because the limits of what can be meaningfully stated has not been understood. The solution is grounded in logic and represented by thought. Propositions of sense – that is, meaningful statements – thought, and the world have the same logical form and therefore the thought and the statement can be pictures of the facts.

Wittgenstein sees the world as consisting of facts, not the traditional view as a world of things. By facts he means existent states of affairs, and these are a combination of objects. An example is a chess piece as an object made of ivory; the state of affairs is the meaningful game, its rules, and the situation in which the object is related. Instead of analyzing the world in which we live as a world of dogs, stars, atoms, ants, clouds, and tables, etc., Wittgenstein points to a world of states of affairs and the totality of these is the world. He is dealing with knowledge and how we come to it. Mostly, since the sixteenth century the questions have been: What is the world out there? And, what is my relation to it?

It seems to me that Wittgenstein is dissolving the opposition of "the world and I" although this is not expressly stated. Against this, he also seems to support Russell's view of reality.

Wittgenstein introduces the notion that thoughts and statements are pictures, pictures of a model reality. To get an idea of this revolutionary document, it needs to be examined methodically. First, its format is unique as a work of philosophy. It consists of 7 statements numbered 1 to 7. Each statement, except 7 is followed by sub-statements, 1.1, then 1.2, etc. There are also sub-sub-divisions, 1.11, 1.111, etc., and also 1.2, 1.21, and so forth, indicating connections between statements. The intention is not to make a new philosophy or amend an existing one. There are no real arguments as the statements are meant to be self-evident. Since all the statements belong together, any selection must fail to do justice to the work. The following extracts can, however, take us into the language and thinking that exemplify this hugely important work, which challenges our conventional ideas on the nature of philosophy and science, as well as morals and aesthetics.

1.   The world is everything that is the case.
1.1   The world is the totality of facts, not of things.
1.11 The world is determined by the facts, and by
      these being "all" the facts.

He investigates how language connects with the real world. When we make statements like "It is raining," we consider that the words and the sentence picture in some way the event out there. Such statements are called propositions and can be either true or false. We also make inferences from such propositions, such as: "It is summer so there will be no snow in Madrid." There are two kinds of inferences, deductive and inductive. Deductive inferences are formally provable from any set of agreed propositions (axioms) whereas inductive inferences rely on statistics or other assumptions as to their universality. Geometry typically employs the deductive and much of science the inductive method.

The language we use can be studied from different aspects. Let us take, for example, "I bought you these flowers," and note how it can be understood in different ways as follows:

Psychology will look at meaning in this statement. How I say it will express different shades of meaning – affection, disappointment, anger or frustration. Philosophy is generally not interested in this aspect.

Epistemology is interested in the correspondence between the thought, the words, and the sentence with what they refer to. It is concerned with how we can know the world or even whether we can know the world as it really is.

Science is concerned with the study of phenomena and coming to an accurate description of these. Russell saw this as establishing the truth or falsehood of statements.

Logic, finally, deals with the relation that the subject of the sentence has to the fact it refers to so as to be capable of being a symbol for that fact. So it is essentially concerned with language as a symbolic expression of reality.

So, any simple statement can be viewed under these different perspectives. The following excerpts from the *Tractatus* indicate its uniqueness:

4.1   Propositions represent the existence and non-existence of states of affairs

4.11   The totality of true propositions is the whole of natural science.

4.111 Philosophy is not one of the natural sciences.

4.112 Philosophy aims at the logical clarification of thoughts. It is not a body of thought but an activity.

4.114 It must set limits to what can be thought and, in doing so, in what cannot be thought.

4.115 It will signify what cannot be said, by presenting clearly what can be said.

Further on we find:

6.52 We feel that even if all *possible* scientific questions be answered, the problems of life have not been answered at all. Of course, there is then no question left and just this is the answer.

6.521 The solution of the problem of life is seen in the vanishing of the problem....

6.522 There are, indeed, things that cannot be put into words. They make themselves manifest. They are what is mystical.

To members of the Vienna School who appreciated much in the content of the rest of the work, the above statements were not readily accepted, and it was suggested they should be scrapped as they spoiled the good.

6.421 It is clear that ethics cannot be expressed. Ethics is transcendental. (Ethics and aesthetics are one.)

This statement has puzzled many commentators. For me, this reveals a sensitivity and level of perception that go beyond referring to rules like 'thou shall" or 'thou shall not." The moral act is not the result of a proposition. It is an insight, which emerges in a situation and, in the moment of the deed, cannot be expressed. Similarly, the moment of aesthetic insight is outside the range of language. It is not surprising that Blake was Wittgenstein's favorite English poet.

After having put out into the world the fruits of his thinking that had ripened in him while an active soldier for four years, he turned his attention to new activities. He gave away his share of the family fortune, became a teacher, a gardener, and an architect. He designed a house in Vienna for his sister.

In 1929, Wittgenstein returned to Cambridge to resume his vocation as a philosopher. His appointment as professor was highly unusual, since he was officially still an undergraduate. This was due to the recognition, which the *Tractatus* had received. Now his thoughts undergo a significant change which also upends his conception of philosophy in its traditional form. He firmly rejects all forms of dogmatism in philosophy and he includes the *Tractatus* as one of them.

From 1930 to 1940, Wittgenstein conducted seminars at Cambridge where he developed most of the ideas that he intended to publish in his second book, *Philosophical Investigations*. He abandoned the study of formal logic and began to examine fallacies in the traditional ways of thinking about language, truth, thought, intentionality, and especially philosophy itself. The book begins with a quotation from the *Confessions of St Augustine*, which describes how the child learns language. This may seem to be a surprising choice as an introduction to a contemporary philosophical text. But surprise with Wittgenstein is no surprise.

> When my elders named some object and accordingly moved towards something, I saw this and I grasped that the thing was called by the sound they uttered when they pointed it out. Their intention was shown by their bodily movements, as it were the natural language of all people: the expression of the face, the play of the eyes, the movements of other parts of the body, and the tone of the voice, which expresses our state of mind in seeking, having, rejoicing or avoiding something.

After I had trained my mouth to form these
signs, I used them to express my own desires.

So why did Wittgenstein put the quote at the beginning of an assault on traditional ways of thinking? The problem is not with Augustine but with the way his seemingly innocent statement was to formulate the questions and answers of philosophy. In other words, because of his standing as a thinker, language has been seen in a particular way, which has shaped philosophy and narrowed our understanding of language.

The *Philosophical Investigations* Part I is made up of 693 numbered statements or aphorisms. Part II was added later and the whole work was published posthumously.

Philosophy has considered its task to explain the way the universe is ordered and in order to do that, it can be set down in propositions. Logic has an essential role in this. The picture of acquiring speech described by Augustine has been taken as a simile of how knowledge is acquired. A main theme of *Philosophical Investigations* is to show the consequences of this approach.

The following citations refer to the fact that Augustine's description of how he learned language has set a false model for philosophy. It has become a way of thinking.

112: A simile that has been absorbed into the forms
of our language produces a false appearance, and
this disquiets us. "But this isn't how it is!" – we
say. "Yet this is how it has to be!"

115: A "picture" held us captive. And we could not
get outside it, for it lay in our language, and language seemed to repeat it to us, inexorably.

The first part of the book deals with language-games. This is the method he developed to explore the nature of language and to dispense with the traditional analytical approach. He begins by imagining a primitive language of four words. The language is used by a builder A and his assistant B who are working with building blocks and have to communicate. B has to pass the blocks in the order A needs them. The words are "block," "pillar," "slab," "beam." A calls out the name of what he wants and B brings the appropriate block. Imagine this as a complete primitive language.

We must imagine this language is the whole language of a tribe. In the tribe, the people are trained to react in this way to the orders of others. In this language-game, language is used to prompt others to do specific things. One can imagine that this basic language might be used in an activity in which some article has to be called over the intercom when needed. In Wittgenstein's scenario, there is just a word and a correct response.

> 7: In the practice of the use of language, one party
> calls out the words and the other acts on them.
> In instruction in the language the following
> process will occur: the learner names the objects,
> that is, he utters the word when the teacher
> points to the stone – and there will be this still
> simpler exercise: the pupil repeats the words
> after the teacher – both of these being processes
> resembling language.

This is the way that Augustine learned to talk. Is it not also the way used in teaching children how to pronounce a word or name an object, but not how to use a term? From this, Wittgenstein imagines other languages. What words signify and how we learn the meaning of language is introduced and will be developed throughout the text.

> 19: It is easy to imagine a language consisting only of
> orders and reports in battle – or a language con-
> sisting only of questions and of expressions for

answering yes or no. And to imagine a language
means to imagine a form of life.

"Language as a form of life." This gives a totally new perspective on language. I grew up speaking a dialect, which we were forbidden to use in school. We accepted this, as I now realize, because the different "forms of life" (a boy with his pals and a schoolchild in a classroom) called for dialect or proper English. The "form of life" is a central feature in the language-game method described below.

Meaning as "use" is also a crucial element in understanding language.

43:     For a large class of cases of the employment of
        the word "meaning" though not for all, this
        word can be explained in this way: the meaning
        of a word is its use in the language.

The following citations from *Philosophical Investigations* will further clarify what Wittgenstein intended by language-games.

23:     The term "language-game" is meant to bring
        into prominence the fact that the speaking of
        language is an activity or form of life.

The list of language-games shows a surprising range including: Reporting an event, speculating about an event, forming and testing a hypothesis, making up a story, reading it, play-acting, singing catches, guessing riddles, making a joke, translating, asking, thanking, and so on.

The list expands our considerations and opens up new possibilities for using and describing language. Each game may have its own rules, unlike the traditional view in which there is one set of rules (use of who and which, for example), and points to the conventional nature of this sort of human activity. In contrast, Wittgenstein avoids imposing any general set of rules on the use of language, which becomes clear in the following.

65:     Here we come up against the great question that lies behind all these considerations. — For someone might object against me: "You take the easy way out! You talk about all sorts of language-games, but have nowhere said what the essence of a language-game, and hence of language, is: what is common to all these activities, and what makes them into language or parts of language. So you let yourself off the very part of the investigation that once gave you yourself most headache, the part about the general form of propositions and of language."

And this is true. – Instead of producing something common to all that we call language, I am saying that these phenomena have no one thing in common which makes us use the same word for all, – but that they are related to one another in many different ways. And it is because of this relationship, or these relationships, that we call them all 'language."

116:     When philosophers use a word – 'knowledge," 'being," 'object," 'I," 'proposition," 'name" – and try to grasp the *essence* of the thing, one must always ask oneself: is the word ever used in this way in the language-game which is its original home? What *we* do is to bring words back from their metaphysical to their everyday use.

By rejecting 'the craving for generality," Wittgenstein points to 'family resemblance" as the more suitable analogy for the means of connecting particular uses of the same word. We should move with the uses of the word through "a complicated network of similarities overlapping and crisscrossing."

Language is an extraordinary phenomenon. It seems to have no boundaries. The little child enters into it, aware that his or her word has meaning and Mum knows it. "Dolly" has a meaning, which may change but the unconscious confidence in language stays as the experience of being human. The poetic nature of language is already the child's experience. A nice example I came across was this remark by a child: A four-year-old called the front of Mum's pointed shoe "the shoe-nose."

Traditionally, grammar-book rules supervise, as it were, what can be said meaningfully and in correct form. But the role of grammar is to express norms or standards so that sentences convey the sense intended. They are a tool to make clear what is muddy. In part II section XI we find:

> I can know what someone else is thinking, not what I am thinking.
>
> It is correct to say, "I know what you are thinking," and wrong to say, "I know what I am thinking."

(A whole cloud of philosophy condensed into a drop of grammar.)

One of the tasks of the *Philosophical Investigations* is to identify the role of philosophy. From Part I:

126: Philosophy simply puts everything before us, and neither explains nor deduces anything. Since everything lies open to view, there is nothing to explain. For whatever may be hidden is of no interest to us.

123: A philosophical problem has the form: "I don't know my way about."

127: The work of the philosopher consists in assembling reminders for a particular purpose.

129: The aspects of things that are most important
for us are hidden because of their simplicity and
familiarity. (One is unable to notice something
because it is always before our eyes.) The real
foundations of his inquiry do not strike a man at
all. Unless that fact has at some stage struck him –
and *that* means we fail to be struck by what,
once seen, is most striking and most powerful.

309: What is your aim in philosophy? – To show the
fly the way out of the fly-bottle.

Philosophical Investigations is non-dogmatic and therapeutic in its
nature, instructing philosophers in the ways of therapy:

133: There is not *a* philosophical method, though
there are indeed methods, like different therapies.

I am interested in the relation of Wittgenstein's philosophy to therapy, though I am not a therapist. It seems to me to offer insights into
the human condition. I came across the work of the therapist, John M
Heaton who has written several books on Wittgenstein and therapy. The
following is a description of his book, *The Talking Cure*, which will give
the reader an understanding of the connection.

Wittgenstein's work on language, the limits of
what can be said, and the expression of thoughts or
failure in senselessness, is used in this book to consider the nature of talking cures. Talking as a way to
help suffering is widespread but Wittgenstein's work
is not another theory depending on certain beliefs.
He rigorously questions our use of language, our
initiation into it that leads to our becoming human
subjects, and the ways we inevitably fall into confu-
sion. Language is both essential to our human way of

life and yet philosophy and therapy are battles against the bewitchment of our intelligence by means of our language. Clarity is obtained through logical analysis, the quiet weighing of linguistic facts, rather than positing empirical entities such as the unconscious to explain loss of reason. What appears to be necessary truths can generate intolerable conflict. So, therapy is concerned to persuade the patient to acknowledge that things need not be as they imagine they must be, or they may be as they imagine they could not be.

Isn't some of the violence of youth in our cities today possibly owed to the inability to express feelings which need to be expressed another way? The undermining of language by loss of vocabulary, especially the vocabulary of feeling, stifles the soul. The story by Herman Melville, of the seaman Billy Budd who strikes and inadvertently kills his false accuser, the Master-at-arms, describes the tragic consequences. Billy lacks the words to tell his side of the story and the captain, although aware of his lack of intent, is obliged by the laws of the navy to hang him.

Philosophical Investigations contains many statements, which stimulate the reader to explore his/her life of thought. We mostly carry a large quantity of assumptions unexplored and in need of examining. Let us consider three more statements from Part I.

335:    Now if it were asked, Do you have the thought before finding the expression, what would you have to reply? And what to the question, What did the thought consist in, as it existed before the expression?

471:    It often happens that we only become aware of the important facts, if we suppress the question "Why?" and then in the course of our investigations these facts lead us to an answer.

570:     Concepts lead us to make investigations, are the
          expression of our interest, and direct our interest.

In the preface to *Philosophical Investigations,* Wittgenstein writes:

> I make them [these remarks] public with mis-
> givings. It is not impossible that it should fall to the
> lot of this work, in its poverty and in the darkness of
> this time, to bring light into one brain or another –
> but, of course, it is not likely. I should not like my
> writing to spare other people the trouble of thinking.
> But, if possible, to stimulate someone to thoughts
> of his own. I should have liked to produce a good
> book. This has not come about, but the time is past
> in which I could improve it.

This shows us the character of the man – modest, severely honest, self-depreciatory. When war broke out, he left Cambridge where he had been made Professor of Philosophy to work as a hospital porter and then in a medical laboratory. He had no attraction to Academia. So many interests occupied him. He was a sculptor, an engineer, an orchestral conductor, and an architect. He made his own furniture and could handle any tool. He could whistle the most difficult symphonies and concertos. He loved the simple life and was admired by the fishermen of the Irish West Coast for his ability to tame wild birds.

Martin Buber (1878 — 1965)

In the first half of the twentieth century, two currents in European philosophy stood apart from each other, even opposed to each other. On the continent, the Existentialist movement, partly inspired by Kierkegaard focused on the experience of the individual in a world generally viewed as hostile to the soul. On the other side of the channel, philosophers were preoccupied with problems of mathematics and logic. The results of science strongly influenced their thinking. The different interests of the two schools were already apparent in the Continental Rationalists and the British Pragmatists.

In this final chapter, our subject, Martin Buber, is one who has his roots in a very different tradition, but was also inspired by Continental thinkers like Ludwig Feuerbach (1804–1872) and Søren Kierkegaard. The book, which he wrote in 1922, *I and Thou,* will be our study and conclude our journey. One may imagine that it was written for 2022, as much of humanity's present struggles seem addressed in Buber's writings. Just over a hundred pages in length, the style is more that of a poetic essay than a philosophical tract. Many of our conventional notions are challenged. Its key theme is "dialogue" and the reality that lives between one and the other.

Vienna was the birthplace of Martin Buber, the city of Wittgenstein and other outstanding figures who shaped the twentieth century. When his parents divorced, he went, at the age of four, to live with grandparents at Lvov in Poland. His grandfather introduced him to the story and the stories of the Hasidim. This was a Jewish sect founded in the middle of the eighteenth century by Baal Shem Tov, an inspired teacher and magic healer who gathered around him disciples dedicated to a life of mystic fervor, joy, and love. Judaism in Eastern Europe had become highly intellectual and remote from the lives of ordinary folk. The heart of this new teaching was not doctrines and sophisticated arguments on the Torah but stories, stories that could bring joy and wisdom. Buber later spent five years studying the Hasidim and found in their history a source of inspiration.

This Hasidic tale will give you their flavor. A young student goes to the door of a rabbi and knocks, and he looks in when the rabbi opens the door, and sees that the room is completely bare, there's no furniture at all, not a skerrick of anything. And the young man says to the rabbi, "Rabbi, where is all your furniture?" And the rabbi says to him, "Well, where is yours?" And the young man says, "But I'm visiting." And the rabbi says, "I'm visiting too."

His grandfather also introduced Buber to the ideas of the Zionist Organization, which debated a return to the ancestral home in Palestine. Reform Jews rejected the idea, but the conviction by a French court of the innocent French officer Dreyfus, who was Jewish, for spying for Germany convinced Theodor Herzl, an Austrian journalist, that a state for the Jewish people was the only answer to European anti-Semitism. From 1900 to 1916 Buber and his life-partner, the author Paula Winkler lived in Berlin. His interests were far reaching. He was master of half-a-dozen languages, and as editor of Herzl's *Die Welt* (The World), he was bathing in all the intellectual hot springs at a time, when in 1914 Europe and then America and Japan plunged into four years of mutual destruction.

Buber expressed to his friend Gustav Landauer his opinion that the war had the virtue of forging a feeling of community in a nation. Landauer was shocked at his friend's "painful and repugnant" thoughts, and this may have awakened in Buber fresh insight into the nature of community. According to Buber, it was about this time that he began to develop thoughts on the theme of *I and Thou*.

I and Thou was translated into English in 1937, and after the war, it had a considerable influence in English-speaking countries. The book begins with the following statements:

> To man the world is twofold, in accordance with
> his twofold attitude. The attitude of man is twofold,
> in accordance with the twofold nature of the primary
> words, which he speaks.

The primary words are not isolated words, but combined words. The one primary word is the combination I-Thou.

The other primary word is the combination I-It; wherein, without a change in the primary word, one of the words He and She can replace It.

Hence, the I of man is also twofold.

For the I of the primary word I-Thou is a different I from that of the primary word I-It.

Primary words do not signify things, but they intimate relations. Primary words do not describe something that might exist independently of them, but being spoken they bring about existence.

Primary words are spoken from the being.

If Thou is said, the I of the combination I-Thou is said along with it.

If It is said, the I of the combination I-It is said along with it.

The primary word I-Thou can only be spoken with the whole being.

The primary word I-It can never be spoken with the whole being.

In recent translations I-You is preferred to I-Thou. I-Thou seems archaic, confined to the seventeenth century. For me, however, I-Thou suggests a quality of relationship that is not so apparent in I-You, hence I will use the former.

The two attitudes, I-Thou and I-It, seem at first like a polarity. Later they seem more like a spectrum reflecting the varied and subtle nature of human relations.

The word "being" is important. It is not a psychological distinction, although he uses the word "attitude." It has an ontological foundation and belongs to the essence of being human.

In the Book of Genesis, God first creates man-woman as the primary unity. Then the dual man and woman are separated in a second act of creation. It is commonly written that Eve is created from Adam's rib, but this translation has been challenged and the Hebrew term also means a "side" (the other side being "male"). So, in the beginning is the primary word I-Thou. In I-Thou there is the home of dialogue. I-It is the world of things that stands against the observing ego. The independent ego emerges from the I-Thou and, as a consequence, relationships with the other, with nature, and with God are changed. Life is an oscillation between the two attitudes. The I-It is the world of space and time, of experience and judgment, of institutions and factories, of objects and of objectifying.

> When Thou is spoken, the speaker has no thing
> for his object. For where there is a thing there is an-
> other thing. Every It is bounded by others; It exists
> only by being bounded by others. But when Thou is
> spoken, there is no thing. Thou has no bounds.

Buber refers to three spheres in which the world of relationship arises. Nature, humanity, and intelligible beings. In the first, the relation "sways in gloom beneath the level of speech"; in the second, human life is where the relation is open and in the form of speech; in the third, that of intelligible beings, "the relation is clouded, yet it discloses itself."

Our relation to nature is almost entirely one of I-It. We may romantically admire it, but it is mostly there for our use and abuse. In human relations, the person gets lost in "the worker," "the Russian," "the immigrant," etc. Buber writes of the "atomization of society," in which Individuals are there to serve society's impersonal needs.

Our contemporary I-It attitude to nature needs no elaboration. Its representation on TV can obstruct our inner relating to the world of animals and plants even when it may show us their wonders. Buber's indications in reference to I-Thou relation to nature is not just appreciation of it; it invites a presence. I regularly take a walk along a tree-lined pathway. It is early spring and green foliage begins to appear at the top of birch and beech and oak and hawthorn. We now know that trees communicate with each other through their roots. A deficiency of an element in one tree can be supplemented from neighboring trees. Each time I take my walk, I have a fresh awareness of the changing life and breath of the community of trees.

The hunter and ecologist Aldo Leopold (1887–1948) describes his experience with a wolf in the American Southwest in his book *The Sand County Almanac.*

Thinking like a mountain

A deep chesty roar echoes from rimrock to rimrock, rolls down the mountain, and fades into the far blackness of the night. There's an outburst of wild defiant sorrow and of contempt for all the adversities of the world. Everything living (and perhaps many a dead one as well) pays heed to this call. To the deer, it's a reminder of the way of all flesh, to the pine, a forest of midnight scuffles and of blood upon the snow, to a coyote, a promise of gleanings to come, to the cowman, a threat of red ink at the bank, to the hunter a challenge of fang against bullet. Yet behind these obvious and immediate hopes and fears, there lies a deeper meaning known only to the mountain itself. Only the mountain has lived long enough to listen objectively to the howl of a wolf.

Those unable to decipher the hidden meaning know nevertheless that it is there, for it is felt in all wolf country, and distinguishes that country from all other land. It tingles in the spines of all who hear wolves by night or see their tracks by day. Even without sight or sound of wolf, it is implicit in 100 small events, the midnight whinny of a pack horse, the rattle of rolling rocks, the bound of fleeing deer; the way shadows lie under the spruces. Only the uneducable tyro can fail to sense the presence or absence of wolves or the fact that the mountain has a secret opinion about them.

So, that's the mountain. And then he tracks a wolf and he sees a wolf and some cubs and he shoots and the wolf is wounded and lies there. And one of the cubs scrabbles away, also wounded. And he goes up to the dying wolf:

> In those days, we had never heard of passing up a chance to kill a wolf. In a second, we were pumping lead into the pack but with more excitement than accuracy; how to aim a steep downhill shot is always confusing. When our rifles were empty, the old wolf was down and a pup was dragging a leg into impassable slide-rocks. We reached the old wolf in time to watch a fierce green fire dying in her eyes. I realized then and I've known ever since that there was something new to me in those eyes – something known only to her and to the mountain. I was young then and full of trigger-itch; I thought that because fewer wolves meant more deer that no wolves would mean hunters' paradise. But after seeing the green fire die, I sensed that neither the wolf nor the mountain agreed with such a view.

We see the other as an object not only out of our egotism but also out of our need. Organizations and all kinds of social structures are necessary. Roles have to be filled, capacities have to be addressed. Assessments of individuals and managing of groups belong to I-It. But we notice that in the twentieth century, also in philosophy, the human being has become an It. The professor observing the table, the door, someone opening the door, then asks, "What is it? Is 'who' so easily reducible? Is it the required attitude of science?" The problem arises when this mode of observing and questioning spreads throughout psychology, social life, and all our thinking.

> The Thou meets us through grace. It's not found by seeking. But my speaking of the primary word to it is an act of my being, is indeed the act of my being. The Thou meets me but I step into direct relationship with it, hence the relation means being chosen and choosing.
>
> All real living is meeting.
>
> Only in "meeting" can the I-Thou relation happen. In I-It there is no present, only the past.

Buber reflects on the nature of love:

> Feelings are "entertained"; love comes to pass. Feelings dwell in man; but man dwells in his love. Love does not cling to the I in such a way to have the Thou only for its object; but love is between I and Thou.

It is clear the English language needs a new word for "man." The Sanskrit word from which man is derived is genderless as in Genesis 1. It is now reserved for the male. "I" has no gender.

"Love is responsibility of an I for a Thou. Relation is mutual. My Thou affects me as I affect it."

In its development, the child meets the world not as object standing against it but in an already existing relation. As the child grows, the I emerges from this relation to meet itself as if it were a Thou. (The child becomes aware of the ego). This separation will eventually establish the I-It relation. In this relation, objects are combinations of qualities. Things are set in space and time, connected by cause, measured, and ordered. But the world that is ordered is not the world-order.

> There are moments of silent depth in which you look on the world-order, fully present. These moments are immortal, and most transitory of all; no content can be secured from them, but their power invades creation and the knowledge of man.

Central to Buber's teaching is the relation to God, the Eternal Thou.

> In the relation with God, unconditional exclusiveness and unconditional inclusiveness are one. He who enters on the absolute relation is concerned with nothing isolated any more, neither things nor beings, neither earth nor heaven; but everything is gathered up in the relation. For to step into pure relation is not to disregard everything but to see everything in the Thou, not to renounce the world but to establish it on its true basis. To look away from the world, or to stare at it, does not help a man to reach God; but he who sees the world in Him, stands in His presence. 'Here world, there God' is the language of It; but to include the whole world in the Thou – this is full and complete relation.

The theme of dialogue occupied Buber during his whole life and he returned again and again to it in his writings. He searched for new ways to describe it. The book *I and Thou* is contradictory, enigmatic and paradoxical, for logical propositions do not capture the flux of human life.

Between Man and Man was published in 1947 and contains the essay "Dialogue" written in 1929. The theme is presented very differently from the 1922 version. It throws a very helpful light in a language perhaps more accessible to the contemporary ear. The essay begins with a remarkable dream (which Buber had frequently) and what it meant for him. Then he shows by example that conversation can be silent and imagines such a situation between two people.

Imagine two people. First one observes the other. As observer, he is intent on fixing the other in his mind. He notes him, writes down his characteristics, and he knows what lies behind them because everyone has been taught what they mean. A face is nothing but physiognomy.

The onlooker is not at all intent in his observation. He just wants a good view to see what will happen. Apart from the initial decision to look, everything else is involuntary. No note taking. No memory-work (forgetting can be good). He trusts that what is worth preserving will be preserved. He notes his impression. What strikes him in the other is not "character" and not "expression." He has the aesthetic view!

Both the observer and the onlooker have a similar orientation. They desire to perceive the person living before their eyes. The person is an object separated from them and their personal life and as a result can be "properly" perceived. Each gathers what he wants but no response or action or demand is expected from the person.

> It is a different matter when, in a receptive hour of my personal life, a person meets me about whom there is something which I cannot grasp in any objective way at all that "says something" to me. This means, speaks something that enters my own life. Perhaps he needs me. Or, it's about myself. The man himself in his relation to me has nothing to do with

what is said. He has no relation to me, he has not noticed me at all. It is not he who says it to me, but it says it.

Buber continues:

> To understand "say" as a metaphor is not to understand it. "Say" refers to real speech. The effect of having this said to me is completely different from that of observing or looking on. I cannot denote or describe the person, in whom, through whom; something has been said to me. This person is not my object; I have got to do something with him. Perhaps to accomplish something about him, perhaps I have to learn something. It is a matter of accepting. The saying may be answered at once or the saying may have a long and manifold transmission before it, and that I am to answer some other person at some other time or place. Now it is only a matter of taking the answering on myself. In each case, a word demanding an answer has happened to me. We may term this way of perception, becoming aware. It does not need to be a person of whom I become aware. It can be a plant, an animal, a stone.

Nothing is excluded. The limits of the possibility of dialogue are the limits of awareness. To be open and to be aware are demanded if the realm of It is to be contained and limited. Buber writes in *Between Man and Man:*

> I have occasionally described my standpoint to my friends as the "narrow ridge." I wanted by this to express that I did not rest on the broad upland of a system that includes a series of sure statements

about the absolute, but on a narrow rocky ridge between the gulfs where there is no sureness of expressible knowledge but the certainty of meeting what remains undisclosed.

Maurice Friedman in his *Life of Buber* comments on this.

> Perhaps no other phrase so aptly characterizes the quality and significance of Martin Buber's life and thought as the one of the 'narrow ridge." It expresses not only 'the holy insecurity" of his existentialist philosophy but also his I-Thou or dialogical philosophy which he formulated as a genuine third alternative to the insistent either-or's of our age. Buber's 'narrow ridge" is no happy middle which ignores the reality of paradox and contradiction in order to escape from the suffering they produce. It is rather a paradoxical unity of what one usually understands as alternatives – I and Thou, love and justice, dependence and freedom, the love of God and the fear of God, good and evil, unity and duality.

In the essay, 'What is Common to All," Buber quotes a saying by Heraclitus whom he describes as the founder of the edifice of Western thought. This fragment is not just a metaphor but is the expression of the direct contemplation of a perceived reality: 'The waking have a single cosmos in common."

Epilogue

WE HAVE NOW COME TO THE END. The end of a journey. On the way we have come across questions, some unexpected, and answers that set new questions. The end is not a finishing point but offers new beginnings.

I have been drawn to the writings of some thinkers more than to those of others. You may also have identified those that speak more directly to you. My attempt has been to understand viewpoints and not to judge them. Just as sympathy for a particular position might undermine critical reflection, so too antipathy can block the path to a deeper appreciation. Taking note of my own inclinations can also help strengthen my understanding.

Philosophy aims at knowing. Knowing demands objectivity. Objectivity will always rely on thinking for a sound foundation. We can hear the claim of our philosophers: "What I have written has a sound foundation in thinking." There will be other elements as well, feelings, intentions, and memories, but thinking cannot avoid the challenge of objectivity.

Certainty is a close ally of objectivity. It has been the central challenge for many philosophers and found diverse arguments. What carried conviction in one period may lack it in another. Indeed, a common basis for proof, even amongst contemporaries, has been fertile ground for disputes and oppositions.

Philosophy is also about meaning and human purpose. Somehow life has to make sense and we look for meaning in things in our everyday. Philosophers focus on large questions, on the nature of the world we dwell in and the nature of the human being.

In the twenty-first century we have arrived at new predicaments on a global scale. The issues that twentieth-century philosophers dealt with can already seem out of date. Traditionally, humanity has seen itself as part of the natural world, although with a special status. Now humanity appears to aim at creating a world in the service of its predetermined needs. These are often shaped by its technological achievements.

In the prologue I introduced the idea of the evolution of consciousness as described by Rudolf Steiner in *The Riddles of Philosophy*. Steiner's description has also accompanied my understanding of each philosopher.

Steiner describes how the Greek thinkers begin to grasp the world in thoughts without pictures. This follows earlier cultures that thought in pictures. At the beginning of the Christian period, there emerged a new self-awareness and a new sense of independence. Augustine is a supreme example of this. The nominalists of the thirteenth and fourteenth centuries mark a clear separation between the outer and inner worlds. "What is going on in my thoughts is independent of what I perceive out there." Concepts have no innate connection with things. They are just labels.

Modern consciousness begins with Descartes and his "I think therefore I am." The natural sciences bring a new consciousness in which nothing from the human soul is allowed to interfere with the understanding of the natural world. The "I" plays no role in the created world except to explain it. It is eliminated from any meaning owed to science. Science has nothing to say about the mystery we encounter when we welcome the little child into the world, when we wonder at nature, when we confront our inner worlds. The human being is simply a biological member of the species, homo sapiens. The advance of modern science and the associated alienation of self from the world is also that which gives to the human spirit a sense of freedom and responsibility that no earlier time could know.

The idea of an evolution of consciousness opens the possibility of as-yet-unknown capacities of the human being. It seems to me to transform our imagination of humanity's future.

In the philosophy of Martin Buber, the I is twofold, I-thou and I-It. Buber maintained that in Western society the I-thou relation has succumbed to or been overcome by the I-it relation. In the I-thou one opens to the other. Reality depends on the meeting in relationship of I and thou.

This understanding bears directly on our society with its widespread mental health problems. Their typical features are anxiety and loneliness.

This story began when I happened on Martin Buber's *I and Thou* and on lectures on education given in England by Rudolf Steiner, found when browsing in a public library. Was It just accidental, or luck? I see it as good fortune. The Roman goddess Fortuna is often shown as blindfolded. She is also shown with a rudder. I go for the rudder. We make many choices in a life. Some choices are our life.

The function of the book is the encounter and its possibilities.

Reading List

PLATO. *Symposium. Republic. Meno.*

ARISTOTLE. *De Anima. Ethics. Metaphysics.*

AUGUSTINE. *Confessions. The City of God.*
    Vernon J Rourke. *Augustine's Quest of Wisdom.*

AQUINAS. *Summa Theologica. On Being and Essence.*
    Matthew Fox. *Sheer Joy.*

BACON. *The Advancement of Learning. Novum Organum. Atlantis.*

DESCARTES. *Discourse on Method. Meditations.*

SPINOZA. *Ethics.*
    Arnold Zweig. *Spinoza.*

LOCKE. *An Essay Concerning Human Understanding.*
    Isaiah Berlin. *The Age of Enlightenment.*

BERKELEY. *A Treatise Concerning the Principles of Human Knowledge.*

HUME. *An Enquiry Concerning Human Understanding.*

KANT. *Critique of Pure Reason. Prolegomena.*
    Stephan Korner. *Kant.*

GOETHE. *Metamorphosis of Plants. The Theory of Color.*
    Henri Borfort. *Goethe's Way of Science.*

HEGEL. *Phenomenology of Spirit. Philosophy of History. Philosophy of Right. Encyclopaedia of the Philosophical Sciences.*
    Werner Hamacher. *Pleroma: Reading in Hegel.*

KIERKEGAARD. *Either/Or. Fear and Trembling. Edifying Discourses (Fontana)*
George Pattison. *Kierkegaard: The Aesthetic and the Religious.*

MILL. *Liberty. Utilitarianism.*

NIETZSCHE. *The Birth of Tragedy. Thus Spake Zarathustra. Echo Homo.*
Karl Jaspers. *Nietzsche et le Christianisme.*

STEINER. *Truth and Knowledge. The Philosophy of Freedom. Friedrich Nietzsche. The Course of My Life.*

HUSSERL. *Ideas II. Cartesian Meditations. Lifeworld.*
Edo Pivcevic. *Husserl and Phenomenology.*

HEIDEGGER. *Being and Time. What Is Called Thinking. The Essence of Human Freedom.*
Julian Young. *Heidegger, Philosophy, Nazism.*
Jeff Collins. *Heidegger.*

RUSSELL. *The Problems of Philosophy. The History of Western Philosophy. Common Sense and Nuclear Warfare. Mysticism and Logic.*

WITTGENSTEIN. *Tractatus Logico-Philosophicus. Philosophical Investigations.*
Ray Monk. *Wittgenstein.*

BUBER. *I and Thou. Between Man and Man. The Knowledge of Man.*
Maurice Friedman. *Martin Buber: The Life of Dialogue*

Acknowledgements

This book would never have appeared without the encouragement of friends and colleagues over many years. What started as a set of introductory talks on philosophical themes presented in Forest Row, Sussex, UK, became the basis for this book. Along the journey key individuals have helped me on my way. I thank and name a few but recognize many more. Jose d'Agostino converted the original recordings of the philosophy talks onto CDs. I have Kim Murriera to thank for reviving interest in the original recordings. Roman Kuznetsov cleaned up the audio quality and converted them to text. Gregers Brinch kindly stepped in to make new recordings to replace inaudible discs. Eric Müller, on hearing the original talks, proposed to publish the work in book form.

I was hesitant. It had been a long time since the talks were given and would they be interesting today? It was Roman's boundless enthusiasm, determination and technical capacities that decided it. We had a publisher and we had to go ahead.

I soon realized that a conversational delivery to an audience of thirty or so in a pub does not convert easily into a publishable text. The talks had to be entirely rewritten. Now the real work began. I could never have managed this without further support from my four children Andreanne, Bernard, Madeleine, and Julian who each played their part in the considerable task of getting the book into shape ready for publishing. While the content was greatly enhanced by their many contributions, any shortcomings are my own.

Lightning Source UK Ltd.
Milton Keynes UK
UKHW022004190122
397393UK00009B/326